THE SWEETEST GAME

Play Golf By Your Better Instincts

———

CAL BROWN

CLOCK
TOWER
PRESS

For information address   Clock Tower Press
                          3622 W. Liberty Rd.
                          Ann Arbor, MI 48103

Cover design by Bruce Worden
Background image from John Notar-Francesco
Foreground image from Corbis

Library of Congress Cataloging-in-Publication Data:

Brown, Cal.
The sweetest game : play golf by your better instincts / Cal Brown.
p. cm.
Includes bibliographical references and index.
ISBN 1-932202-20-X
1. Golf—Miscellanea. I. Title.
GV967.B86 2004
796.352—dc22
2004016322

To Denise St. Jean,

A woman for all seasons

CONTENTS

INTRODUCTION

Like any other golfer, I've thought about the game and the golf swing until the mind blanked, and had a hundred epiphanies and a thousand brilliant insights. All of them seemed perfectly sensible at the time, but none really worked. The game is wicked. It is possible that some of you who glance through this book may not have discovered this, but you will.

The search for the secret swing knowledge of the game's masters—that of Harry Vardon, Bobby Jones, Ben Hogan, Jack Nicklaus, and Tiger Woods—has always been an honorable part of the game, even though we know that those secrets and the talent that informs them are not ours to capture entirely. Still, we pursue them and discover that some of the insights, though not the talent, offered by the masters can indeed be ours. We learn valuable, practical knowledge from them that allows us to improve our own golf. These insights are at the heart of this book, using common sense and humor to cast light on some fairly simple ideas about playing golf for pleasure.

This book suggests another way of looking at the game and the golf swing that doesn't use so much technical jargon or dark secrets and instead relies more on making do with your natural abilities and tendencies. These are worth more than you think. The book is also about the joys, the sorrows, the hopes, the little horrors, the temptations, and the uncounted satisfactions of golf. The chapters are arranged in a roughshod kind of order, and they can be read straight through, or just as easily by opening the book and starting to read anywhere.

I've chosen to quote Harry Vardon, among other ancients, at length to bring us back to his phrases and acknowledge an almost forgotten genius to generations that never knew him, because his ideas are sound. Golfers can study these phrases with both delight and insight. The same can be said for old crocks like Taylor, Park, and Simpson, along with dear old Darwin and the rest of that musty crowd, many of whom we can listen to with profit. Then there's the obvious reason—that most of the ideas we think of as new in golf have been around since Lincoln lived in the White House. Despite superplastics, titanium, and trampoline effects, there isn't much new in the old game except that we can now gratify our lust for distance so much more easily.

Although often wicked, golf is the sweetest game, because it affords us endless opportunities to imagine ourselves geniuses, to chase risk, to dream of glory, and sometimes to reach our goal. Anyone who has hit a sweet shot knows the feeling. It also tempts us to return to try again and again. With the sweet comes its unavoidable twin, the bitter. We understand golf well enough to swallow the irritations of a shabby performance even as we scheme for success the next time. This usually leads to the bitter pill known as golf instruction.

Cal Brown
Juno Beach, Florida
April, 2004

CHAPTER
ONE

INSTRUCTION IS A BORE

---

*"If they taught sex the way they teach golf, the human
race would have died out long ago."*
—Jim Murray

Let's be honest, golf instruction is a bore.

Walter Hagen and Gene Sarazen didn't believe in it. Neither did
Ben Hogan or Sam Snead or Paul Runyan or Lee Trevino. Rough
types, those fellows, who sought their own light and dug their
swings out of the dirt, as Hogan liked to put it. Their own patch
of dirt. On the other hand, you may have noticed they were not
above imparting their golf wisdom to others, particularly when
they could make money from it. Hagen and Sarazen did, so did
Runyan and Snead. Even Hogan did. When Henry Luce, the
boss at Time Inc., threw a few thousand bucks his way, Hogan
grabbed it.

1

Others thirsted for it, though. Alister Mackenzie, the golf course architect, turned himself from a hopeless dub into a passable golfer by following the tuition of Ernest Jones, an English pro who lost a leg in World War I and so became a golf teacher. Tom Kite went through most of the canon of modern golf teaching, notwithstanding that he was a genius to start with. Kite will admit that he earnestly pursued the teachings of Harvey Penick, Bob Toski, Labron Harris, Jimmy Ballard, Manuel De La Torre, Paul Bertholy, Jim Flick, Davis Love Jr., Rick Smith, Chuck Cook, Hank Haney, Jack Lumpkin, and others he may have forgotten. Tom is one of those detail-oriented golfers who has always been afraid one of these gurus might harbor a secret he hadn't heard about. Ben Crenshaw, who grew up with Kite in Austin, Texas, was the opposite. It's not certain that Ben actually took formal golf lessons, at least not until recently, and he listened only to one coach, Harvey Penick. Different strokes.

Golfers bored with instruction can take inspiration from immortals like these three (L-R) Ben Hogan, Paul Runyan and Lee Trevino, none of whom had the benefit of golf lessons. Hard cases all, they dug their swings out of the dirt; but mind you, they worked for it.

Golf instruction is a bore because it takes time away from the good stuff, like crushing a tee shot and watching the ball soar 280 yards—or in your dreams, if you're like most of us. Some folks can't exactly do that, nor roll the ball along the ground with much confidence when the object is the hole. Which is why they seek golf instruction. It can't be that hard to hit a motionless ball that's sitting there waiting to be hit. No, you wouldn't think so, and that's where all the trouble starts.

Physically and mentally, golf is a game of reaction, not action. Every swing is based upon the memory of impact—not a general impression of it, but a specific memory of the last one. If my previous shot went to the right, my instincts will combine to see that I don't hit the next one there. This happens automatically because our brains and synapses are programmed to react to things, a fundamental and very useful survival mechanism. I don't think golfers can change this, and wouldn't gain much even if they

Harvey Penick, the great teacher from Austin, Texas, is flanked by two of his brightest pupils, Tom Kite (left), a fellow who thirsted after golf instruction, and Ben Crenshaw, a fellow who didn't.

wanted to. In a way, I suppose that's all golf is, a bit of survival from one stroke to the next and on to the objective. Still, these reactions are what lead us to seek the magic cures we have heard about. After all, we did not intend to slice the ball into the woods, and we will bloody well know both the reason and the cure. This is part of what we fight and is why we seek instant corrections to the thousand little misdemeanors we commit during the course of a round. Down that path lurks temporary relief, but more often, as the old storyteller warned, there be dragons and demons and tangled nests.

John Henry Taylor, an ancient figure nowadays, remains an honored legend for his link with Harry Vardon and James Braid as one of The Great Triumvirate. Taylor grew up in Northam, in North Devon, England, where he attended school with Rudyard Kipling. In a letter to Taylor long after the great golfer had won

J. H. Taylor, the first of golf's Great Triumvirate to win the Open Championship, (at Royal St. George's, Sandwich, England in 1894) played with a natural, determined style that eventually carried him to five Open titles.

the fifth of his British Open Championships, Kipling recalled their teenage adventures, writing in part: "We golfed where and when we chose and there were very few books or theories to confuse the mind or the muscles." To Taylor, this was "a very shrewd and true observation and one with which I agree." Much has happened since those days to change the implements and playing fields of the game. Information and knowledge have grown enormously, and technique has probably improved a thousandfold. In the spread of all this knowledge I wonder if we're not overlooking those elements of mind and muscle Kipling wrote about and about which Taylor and many of his successors remind us.

No two men knew more about hitting a ball with a stick than Sam Snead, The Slammer, and Ted Williams, The Thumper, although in different games. The two shared a passion for fishing and used to go after bonefish in the Florida Keys. During one expedition, they had a famous dispute about which was tougher to hit—a baseball or a golf ball. Snead said: "You've got eight other men on your side, and you get to hit maybe four times in a game. Why, in golf, we're all by our own selves, and we gotta hit about seventy balls and walk pret' near a mile and a half."

"Aaaaah, bull," Ted replied. "You're hitting a round ball with a square club, you got it all teed up nice, just sitting there waitin' to be hit, and you can swing whenever you feel like it. Now, we use a round bat and that ball ain't sitting there waitin' for us, it's coming at us about ninety to a hundred miles an hour. You can't tell me it's not harder to hit a baseball than a golf ball."

Sam paused, and a sly grin appeared: "Maybe it isn't, but when we hit a foul ball, we gotta go find it and then play it!" And that was the end of the debate.

Sam Snead (left) and Ted Williams (center) and bridge player Charles Goren prepare for an expedition to the Florida Keys, a favorite haunt of the two sportsmen, who sometimes argued about which was harder to hit, a golf ball or a baseball.

There, in a nutshell, is the wicked source of our frustration and fascination with golf. We have to go find the ball and play it. Books and magazines are filled with wildly varied and often confusing advice on how to learn the golf swing. Not many tell you about the game itself, which is a pity because the golf swing is relatively easy to learn, while the game is not. The confusion arises because we are all different—different bodies, different temperaments, different attitudes, different sizes and shapes. The most useful physical attributes in golf are hand- eye coordination, balance, and something called "feel," which most athletes—whether billiard players or race car drivers or basketball players—but not all citizens, possess to a more or less blessed degree.

Golf instructors know this and, while genuinely seeking to improve the lot of their pupils, spend largely unprofitable (for the pupil) weeks or months trying to compensate for a student's lack of coordination or balance by prescribing sometimes intricate and tedious drills. These drills are not harmful in themselves, but neither are they particularly helpful unless the pupil suffers from a physical disability, perhaps, or a mental one—like impatience. Greed and impatience and unbridled arrogance are enemies to the game of golf, as all the great players have learned at their cost. This is not to say that mercy and humility are the secrets to winning golf, else Jack Nicklaus and Sam Snead would not have become the champions they were. On the other hand, when golfers, even the great ones, say, "It's a humbling game," they mean it because they know it. So, wherein lies the lure of the game?

GOLF'S APPEAL AND OBSESSIONS

Clues to understanding the appeal, some would say the obsessions, of golf can be found by looking to its origins. A gorgeously expensive book appeared recently that traces the history of golf largely through art. After a bit of dodging, it concludes that golf evolved in France in the district of Loire. Pretty book, but not very likely. What follows are notions of what may have led up to golf's origins. Historians would have every right to wince at the sort of inductive reasoning used. On the other hand, it explains things about the game that are peculiar to it and to the culture that bred it, and offers an insight into why golfers continue to search for glory.

Games with balls and sticks have been around since cavemen swatted their opponents' skulls across ditches, and have been part of nearly every culture in human history. Nothing new there, but historians suggest that the Romans played a form of golf before the Dark Ages, that the Dutch and now the French or the Flemish followed somewhat later than that, and I've even read that the Chinese were wielding something that looked suspiciously like golf implements while trotting around their courtyards in the tenth century or thereabouts. Fat chance. I have no idea who came up with the idea of knocking rocks and sheep droppings across the open downs and moors with wooden canes, but there can be no doubt that the game as we know it was fully developed in Scotland. You have only to look at the early playing fields and acquaint yourself with golf's original rules to know this.

Where else could the game have emerged? It would not have occurred to anyone living in a forest to invent golf, nor to hit rocks around the edge of a lake. To what purpose? It is unlikely that those living in steep or hilly terrain would have bothered to chase rocks or balls up and down hill, and in those days the common folk were far too sensible to put flat, fertile farmland to any other use. No, it is quite clear that golf could not have arisen anywhere but Scotland, and nowhere else but on the rugged and otherwise unused downs or links land beside the seashore.

Bear in mind that the Celts were always a belligerent race who loved nothing so much as a quarrel, and who sought their grudges everywhere. Daily armed combat was a staple of the Pict culture as well, centuries before the Romans invaded the misty isle they called Albion with its wild inhabitants in the north, a region the Romans named Caledonia, and the brutish Scots joined in willingly when they arrived from their original home in Ireland. Dirks, fists, and claymores were the favored tools. They would carve a limb from a man's body without a care, pillage a town for an afternoon's entertainment, and the stuff they ate is scarcely imaginable.

Contrary to what you may have heard, the Picts and Scots were not drawn to notions of brotherhood. Clans were fiefdoms, not family collectives. In Gaelic, the word "clan" means child, and the chiefs treated their "clansmen" accordingly. They were overbearing, murderous louts who won their positions by mortal combat or assassination, then held it by the same means. They treated their "clans" as chattel, property rightfully earned, and slaughtered those who supposed otherwise.

To earn a place at the table, a man developed what combative skills he could and learned to put personal discomfort aside. No quarter was asked, none given. The climate was cold, wet, angry, and harsh, qualities that molded the people and the pastimes they developed. Games of swordplay, spears, caber tossing, and heaving great, heavy stones were popular among this crowd. Amidst the rocky mists and gales of the Highlands and across the bleak, wind-whipped open downs and moors along the sea, the second greatest pleasure a man could find was in besting the thrusts of Mother Nature. A game that offered an easy route to the target would have held no fascination for these rowdy creatures, and surely would have perished.

In warfare, the Scots were not particularly interested in large maneuvers. Individual combat was the thing; close with the enemy as quickly as possible and stare him in the eye before bludgeoning the silly wretch. If the Picts ventured occasionally into group mayhem, they stripped and painted their bodies a startling shade of blue and attacked on the run with fierce screams and rage. It was common for a smaller band to overwhelm a superior force by fright and intimidation.

Very early on, these ruffians learned to intimidate opponents with their disturbing appearance and behavior. This was among the earliest examples of psychological warfare, and rather successful it was. Using these primitive techniques, they kept the much better equipped Romans and, later, the English and Norse, at bay for several centuries. From this heritage, too, grew a race of independent, self-reliant brutes whose swagger was typically expressed by the Scottish notion of "having a good conceit of yourself." Is anything more useful to success in the game?

So there they were, rough, belligerent men with a fierce love of man-to-man combat, expert gamesmen, masters of devious tactics, a race that took its hardships raw and loved it, wild and clever creatures who had no choice but to pit their best against nature's worst. Think on this for a moment. Can we imagine the practical, mercantile Dutch or the subtle, urbane French, or the wary, land-poor Flemish developing a game that so keenly embraces those fierce, uncompromising qualities and large spaces? Look to the game, man, to its rules. Touch the ball between tee and hole and the wager is lost. Probably a hand, too. Strike fairly and count each one if you value your honor, or your limbs.

The contest between one man and another, the Scots' preferred style, eventually evolved into competitions in which winner and loser were determined by counting the total number of strokes. But that came later; the first rules were straightforward, uncompromising, and fair, much like the Scottish character itself, and embraced a hostility to change that was, as historians have noted, an instinctive trait of many Scots. Those few, simple rules would be corrupted, of course, when the English and the Americans eventually got hold of them.

As the game developed, so did the ecclesiastic influences in Scotland, perhaps coincidentally. While the affects of this sort of piety on the Scottish soul are believed to have calmed the savage instinct somewhat, the melancholy depths of the national spirit persisted, and these conflicting strains were absorbed into the game we now call golf. Of that there can be no possible doubt. Robert Louis Stevenson was a Scotsman who followed pursuits other than golf, but the national ethos resonates in his line, quoted at the head of Chapter Five: "Our business in life is not to succeed, but to continue to fail in good spirits."

One thing more. The game was born in sand. That marvelous substance, so grainy and porous, has had an irresistible influence on the game's evolution.

The game was born in sand, a setting very much like this one from Prestwick in 1889. In the early days, manicured fairways and greens were largely unknown. The bearded fellow watching in the center is Old Tom Morris.

It was the medium upon which the first playing fields were laid out among the whins and gorse bushes and grasses that grew along the seacoast. When weather or animals scratched a bare spot, the sandy base was revealed in an infinite variety of shapes and sizes according to nature's whims. These were the first natural hazards, some shallow scoops and others deep pits, and they became another of the game's obstacles. Sand and sand bunkers influenced the rules of the game as well as the layout and contours of the holes. The very resilience and permeability of sand allowed the playing fields to be placed where most convenient, and for the game to be played pretty much the year around.

Putting greens bore no resemblance to the smooth surfaces of today. They were barely more than spaces cleared around the holes, crude scrapings in the sandy scrub. Eventually these clearings grew larger and smoother, but over decades, perhaps centuries. Even then, the early implements had to have a good bit of loft just to get the balls to scamper across the rough surfaces. Turf flourished on the sandy soil without human aid, fueled by mists and rains, while rabbits, field mice, gulls, and owls swooped and ran wild over the ground, supplying the odd bits of fertilizer, and there is fairly good anecdotal evidence that domestic sheep and goats were an aid in this and in keeping the turf well trimmed. To a thrifty race, there could not have been a more satisfactory arrangement.

Recall, too, that those hazards of theirs were called "sand bunkers" not tulip beds, as they might have been had the game arisen in Holland. The Dutch were clever entrepreneurs and commercial geniuses, and pretty good with dikes and ice skates, but their sporting instincts were somewhat less strenuous than those needed for golf and archery. Their Flemish cousins, on the other hand, acquired the arts of finance and cartography through imitation and proximity to power. Maps and banking yes, golf no. As for the French, I leave it for you to decide.

And the English? Well, we know about them, don't we? Themselves a hopeless tangle of races, they practiced war and mayhem with tenacious and bloody sincerity while coveting the lands of the wild tribes to their north. Shooting, drinking, and the odd theatrical production were about the limits of their recreational imagination. For several hundred years the English attitude to anything produced in Scotland, with the possible exception of "the creature," (a pet name for the native beverage, whisky, which is derived from the Gaelic word meaning "water") was summed up in Samuel Johnson's roundly dismissive quote: "The noblest prospect which a Scotchman ever sees is the high road that leads him to England." That was one of those occasions when Dr. Johnson's prejudice overran his judgment. His countryman Winston Churchill was more generous to the

A rare photo of a fellow who despised all games, including golf, is seen with club in hand in 1913 when he was First Lord of the Admiralty. Though Winston Churchill didn't think much of golf, he admired the Scots.

Scots, saying that among the small nations of the earth, only the Greeks have contributed more to mankind, although golf, I gather, was not among the gifts he had in mind. One of them became America's most cherished symbol, the dollar sign, which was invented at St. Andrews University. In any event, England is an unlikely candidate as golf's birthplace.

A German historian recently claimed he had found evidence that golf originated in Holland and migrated to Scotland in the fourteenth or fifteenth centuries when trade flourished between the two countries. He based his evidence on artwork showing a form of hockey played on ice. For many years, prints of the original paintings by Adriaen Van de Velde and Antonie Van Straelen depicting this game on ice have hung in my living room, mainly because they are attractive and well-detailed. In these pictures, the game looks as much like golf as bocce with a stick. An official of the Royal and Ancient Golf Club of St. Andrews has pointed out a practical flaw in this theory: "The Dutch did indeed play a game with a ball and stick, but there was no hole, and if there's no hole, there's no golf." That sounds reasonable.

The German historian doesn't mention temptation, either. As every golfer knows, the whole business of temptation is central to the appeal and the strategy of the game. I'll probably get in trouble for saying so, but while the Old Testament and the Quran say temptation is among the roots of evil we know, don't we, that golf provides an opportunity to indulge it without damaging one's immortal soul. The Scots tumbled to this almost immediately, and no race has been more deeply imbued with righteous, if belligerent behavior. Who would know more about moral consequences than this bunch whose entire history has been marked by religious wars and parochial conflicts arising from mostly sincere, devout beliefs? Who else would have so enthusiastically welcomed the chance to indulge a temptation or two when the consequences were so obviously immediate rather than eternal? No, it was Scotland, all right.

For some reason, the historical records that might shed light on the origins and early history of golf have yet to be uncovered. I keep waiting for someone to find a stone tablet in a monastery, or a quarto of dusty municipal records forgotten in an attic that could provide us with proper clues to the game's provenance. Something is bound to turn up sooner or later. Until then, I'll be content with an explanation like the one suggested here, in which the game is seen to arise out of the impulses of the men in whose culture and natural world it was so providentially found. Had it been found anywhere else, what a dreary game it might have been.

GOLF IS SELDOM WHAT IT SEEMS

As most players discover, golf is chiefly a mental and an emotional game, not a physical one. The great English teacher John Jacobs maintains that hitting golf shots is fairly simple, but playing golf is very difficult indeed. Those who have trouble with their golf shots, whether occasionally or regularly, will search for another way to strike the ball. Often the cure is rather simple— ball position, posture, a subtle change in grip position or pressure—and can be fixed in minutes.

We will explore in some detail what each of us can do, regardless of our talent, that will allow us to enjoy the game a little more. That is all most of us seek. It may cheer you to know this is not an instruction book. I wouldn't know what to tell you, or how to express it. These ramblings are intended to help you figure things out for yourself. Teaching the usual mechanics of golf are the jobs of professional teachers, and are best left to them.

The scope here is more general and practical, and the hope is that you may find a bit of self-confidence in a game that doesn't offer a lot. If you can hit a perfectly dreadful shot and not be completely humiliated but rather learn something from it, you are well ahead of the game. John Jacobs is fond of saying that the best teacher is the golf

John Jacobs, the tall Englishman who was founder of the modern European PGA Tour and its first Director General, a former Ryder Cup player and captain of two Ryder Cup teams, is also a seminal figure in golf teaching.

ball; how it flies will tell you exactly what has transpired in your golf swing. If you doubt it, you may be ignoring simple cause and effect. The second best teacher—and surely the best learner—is the golfer himself. The noted graphic designer Alexey Brodovitch was once sought as an instructor, and responded: "I am not a teacher. I can irritate and intrigue you, but you must teach yourself." That's the best any good "teacher" can do, whether it's golf or graphics.

A gentle word here. Almost anything that follows is better taken with a grain of salt; none of it is meant to be taken as gospel. If your game still doesn't work after finding a nugget or two that appeals to you, I can tell you what Jacobs would say. Whenever a pupil grew impatient, John would smile sweetly and purr: "Cheer up, the first ten years are the worst!" That, dear friends, is golf, and whatever else it may be, it is never boring.

Chapter Two

The Temptations of Golf

"Why, sometimes I've believed as many as six impossible things before breakfast." —Lewis Carroll

Some golf teachers and not a few golfers believe that the temptations of golf may transcend those in the Garden of Eden. How true it seems, and how devious those temptations can be. The first and most diabolical is the temptation to hit farther. And farther. And farther. There is no end to it. Consider that the farther one hits a golf ball with flush contact, the more urgent is the call to hit harder and thereby to exert even more effort on each successive swing. This goes on with sweet delight as each successive shot rises higher and flies farther, until the moment the system fails and all of it disintegrates into a pathetic pool of jelly.

Why is this so? Can we not be satisfied with a long, powerful drive? With one that goes exactly where we aim it? No, of course we can't. We must surpass ourselves. The ego swells with each majestic stroke. We are convinced that the secret is ours, and nothing stands in the way of immortality. Fool! Dolt! Do you not recognize this driveling wretch?

Listen to one of the greatest ball strikers in history: "The man who has never stood upon the tee with a sturdy rival near him and driven a perfect ball, the hands having followed well through and finished nicely up against the head, while the little white speck in the distance, after skimming the earth for a time, now rises and soars upwards, clearing all obstacles, and seeming to revel in its freedom and speed until at last it dips gracefully back to earth again—I say that the man who has not done this has missed one of the supreme exhilarations of life. There are very few joys in the world of sport that can be compared with it, and none that is superior."

Harry Vardon wrote that, and who would have known the sensation better than he? There we have the clue to the tempting treachery itself. The same Vardon could write: "I must warn the golfer against a constant attempt, natural but very harmful, to drive a much longer ball every time than was driven at the previous stroke. He must bring himself to understand that length comes only with experience, and that it is due to the swing becoming gradually more natural and more certain." How neatly he puts it.

Beware, though. Contrary to most of what we read in the golf magazines, it's pretty clear that golf is a game of feel and emotion, not one of perfect positions and correct moves. The trouble with this is that feel cannot be taught, only experienced, and sometimes, with the judicious application of time, acquired. Emotion is emotion, sisters and brothers, and that is that. The old adage might well read, "Vanity, thy name is golfer." In truth, we are all vain creatures, particularly men when it comes to physical prowess. We find it difficult to accept failure in what we perceive as

Harry Vardon was the leading light in an age of great golfers, and wrote about the game with skill and insight. He was one of the first, but not the last to warn of the devious, wicked temptations of golf.

the relatively undemanding skills needed for golf. Yet the act of striking a golf ball is within the grasp of anyone, even those handicapped by loss of limbs or even sight. There are countless examples. This is because golf is largely played by instinct, aided only by our wit. It requires adopting only a few rudimentary principles to achieve correct impact of club against ball so that the ball travels forward and eventually goes in the hole. With the possible exception of distance—and even here there are plentiful examples of short hitters becoming champions—golf is, physically, a fairly simple business.

So why do we go wrong so often? Is it vanity alone that makes it easier to blame externals for our failures rather than to seek the correction within ourselves? Books and films and countless teaching centers provide a rich choice of technical dogma to choose from, but historically, there has been little apparent agreement among the many competing systems and theories. So we can flit from one to another like a bee from flower to flower, ever hopeful we'll locate truth. The difference is that the bee knows what it's after because Mother Nature has provided the needed instincts. As golfers, I wonder if we might not be better off if we had something of the same.

We face as well the temptation to dream about posting a great score rather than playing the next hole or next shot. Don't we remember Hogan's admonition that the most important shot in golf is the next one? We get so caught up in posting a good score on one or two holes that we imagine ourselves marching to the ninth green with a short putt for thirty-two and the gallery's admiration. Or we picture a long iron drawn majestically to the flagstick, and then forget to aim the silly thing. Distraction is a wicked partner of golf's temptations.

During nearly ten years of toiling in the tiny cubicles at *Golf Digest*, I was doomed to inherit the instruction beat for a time where I had little choice but to write and edit a few instruction books and far too many instruction articles for this otherwise splendid magazine. These and other later features compiled for other publications were written under the rubric of or about Doug Ford, Billy Casper, Bob Toski, Harvey Penick, Cary Middlecoff, Paul Runyan, Gene Sarazen, Eddie Merrins, Sam Snead, John Jacobs, Jerry Barber, Ken Venturi, Mike Souchak, Bob Goalby, Jim Flick, Peter Thomson, Dave Marr, Gardner Dickinson, Davis Love Jr., Ernie Vossler, Ben Crenshaw, and some others.

In addition, I was assigned for several years as the director of the magazine's instruction schools, a position for which I was blissfully unqualified. Never mind, said the owners, you are earnest and cheaply bought. So off I went to the practice pastures of American golf where I was obliged to observe golf teaching at first hand by some of those professionals. To my mind, that is the most intense form of teaching imaginable, because the instructors are under orders to produce results on contract, as it were, in six days with largely unpromising material—hopeless dubs, hopeful beginners, and, dreariest of all, a procession of high-powered business executives who long ago had lost the blessed capacity to listen.

Listening is something a writer does by instinct and training, and so does the manager of such an operation if he wants the customers to return. For several years I listened and watched. I could marvel at the ability of, say, a Bob Toski to intuitively zero in on the core problem in a golfer's technique, or the gentle wizardry of a Harvey Penick as he spread his smooth mixture of honey and wisdom over a pupil's uncertainty, or the quick, certain diagnosis

The early spread of golf in America owes much to men like Jack Burke (above left, giving son Jack Burke Jr. a swing tip), who went from caddie to top pro and moved from Philadelphia to Texas in the late 1910s, and Willie Hunter (above right), who not long after emigrated from England to Los Angeles where he set up shop at Riviera.

by a John Jacobs—sometimes without even looking at the golfer but instead watching the ball flight—and the equally effective cure delivered with unmistakable authority and accuracy.

Through all of this listening and watching, two things gradually became clear to me. First, it is always useful to listen to a first-class player's thoughts about playing the game (and, if you are lucky, to watch him, or her, do it). Mind you, I said "player," not "instructor," because I can recall only one or two grand exceptions to the rule that great players make the best teachers. The reason is that first-class players *know* the way it feels and the

Other major influences in golf teaching included Alex Smith (above left) who came with his brothers Willie and Macdonald from Carnoustie and settled in New York, and Bob MacDonald (above right), a native of Dornoch who emigrated to Buffalo, and then Chicago. All were first rate players who became influential teachers.

devious ways the mind can be made to defer to emotion. Their experience has taught them the errors of many false paths, and their success is sufficient warrant of authority.

This has been true since golf came to America. Once here, it quickly spread to all regions and instruction followed the popularity of the game, shaped and influenced by first-class players like Alex Smith in New York, Jack Burke Sr. in Texas, Willie Hunter in Los Angeles, and Bob MacDonald in Chicago. Many were native Scots, and instruction was given in person. Later, magazines and movies provided wider and cheaper distribution of instruction ideas, although the explanations and images were once removed, and often muddled. The editorial arts improved, but the difficulty has remained.

That brings me to the second point: Most of the stuff we read in golf magazines and watch on television is drivel. This is hard to admit because I was for so many years among the purveyors of this drivel. It's not easy to convey golf instruction using only the two-dimensional limits of golf magazines, books, and television. Sometimes a swing thought can be suggested by a written or spoken word that may actually lead the reader or viewer in the right direction. Other times, it may cause harm because there will be no one standing by to correct the poor sod who has taken the advice as gospel. However, these are irresistible temptations. Who can blame us for watching and hoping to catch a miracle?

Not long ago, Arnold Palmer was asked to comment on the state of teaching and teaching pros: "There's not enough emphasis on fundamentals, grip, stance, head position, that sort of thing," Arnold said. "I cringe when I hear a golf pro tell a weekend golfer how the various parts of his body should behave at the start of the golf swing, or how he should move laterally, or a hundred other things. That's too much information; it's beyond the student's capabilities. I believe in my father's philosophy: Don't try to make a fur coat out of a sow's ear."

Arnold can be forgiven a butchered aphorism because he's telling us to pay attention to what is important—how to hold the club, and to keep the rest simple.

An ideal approach to learning the game, then, might be to give beginners a reasonably sound grip and set them on their way without all the confusing swing theory and technical mumbo-jumbo that only tempts the rest of us. Happily, such a learning path exists. As far as I know, it was devised by Bob Toski during his formative years as a teaching pro following his premature retirement from competitive golf in the late 1950s. He left the tour shortly after his grand victory in the World Championship of Golf, which then offered the richest prize in golf.

Toski took up the noble profession in Miami and soon settled at the Ocean Reef Club, a fashionable resort in the Florida Keys, where he learned how difficult the teaching game could be. His pupils seemed unable to grasp the simplest notion of getting a golf ball to travel along the line of play. This was a first principle enunciated by a Scottish-American teacher

Bob Toski, a member of the World Golf Teaching Hall of Fame, retired in the late 1950s while in his prime as a player and turned to teaching, where he soon stumbled upon an elegantly simple method of showing pupils how to play golf.

named Seymour Dunn, a nephew of Young Willie Dunn, who was involved with the design of the original Shinnecock Hills course and won the first, though unofficial, U. S. Open Championship in 1894. Young Willie also finished second to Englishman Horace Rawlins in the official inaugural played at Newport,

Seymour Dunn (at right) is shown at Saranac, N.Y. in 1923 with Jock Hutchison, winner of the 1920 PGA Championship and 1921 British Open. Dunn published an important instruction book in 1922 that influenced many later teachers, including Bob Toski.

Rhode Island, in 1895. Seymour Dunn became a well-known teacher in Manhattan and published one of the earliest, rather technical books on golf in the United States. Many of Dunn's ideas found their way into Toski's teaching, including the notion of "the line of play."

How often we get tied up in learning to swing and to hit rather than learning how to *PLAY* golf. As Toski thought about this and about Dunn's principle, it gradually dawned on him that the best way to teach would be to start the student close to the hole itself. Placing the pupil's golf ball a few inches from the hole, Bob would ask him or her to knock it into the hole. That was easy. Gradually, Bob would move the ball back from six to twelve inches, with the same instruction: "Knock it into the hole." The only suggestions he made were to hold the club with the palms more or less opposed, as we do when we make a full swing, to keep the hands and arms relaxed, and to imagine a swinging stroke rather than a jab or stab. As his pupils moved farther from the hole, Toski encouraged them to hole at least half the strokes taken from each distance they tried. This built confidence as well as a sense of rhythm and balance. As the distance increased, so did the arc of the swing. This was natural rather than contrived, they learned. Pretty soon, the pupils were at the edge of the green where they noticed that the putter was beginning to swing higher, too. Here Toski handed them a more lofted club; his sole instruction was that they make the same basic swing, only longer to account for the greater distance needed. The loft of the club, pupils learned, took care of getting the ball airborne long enough to carry over the fringe at the edge of the green.

Ideally, the pupils would move father back only when they had gained confidence in playing shots from a particular distance. As they moved back to the fairway, Toski explained, the arc of the swing becomes longer, just as they had experienced on the green itself, to account for the greater distance needed and also to provide enough loft to carry the ball onto the putting surface. If pupils got in trouble, Toski moved them closer to the green to rekindle a sense of confidence and of the swing pace required for that distance. This went on until a pupil grew confident hitting a wedge with a rather full swing. Not much time was spent on technicalities. Toski focused on the important object of getting the ball to land on the green and roll toward the cup.

The effect of this approach, as Toski well knew, built a successful feel in the golfer for the forces and directions of a successful golf swing, and did it without complicated swing theories or explanations. Perhaps just as important, his approach offered unskilled golfers a straightforward way to develop a sense of hand-eye coordination, one of the most useful assets for golf.

"In golf, the eye perceives, the mind receives, and the body reacts," Toski has observed. "To play golf successfully, the eyes have to see the target, and they have to aim the club at the target, and this is done with the hands."

In this classroom, everything is right there in front of the golfer. Tap the ball into the hole from four inches—anyone can do that. Move it back to six, then twelve inches, and tap it in from there, and then try from two feet, then three feet, and on. The feeling builds, the swings become longer, the shots land on the green and roll toward the target. Pretty soon, confidence builds using full swings, and the golfer can progress from nine-iron to eight, to seven, and so on into the middle irons and then the longer clubs. Sure, more instruction is required at this stage, but the most important lessons have been learned—a feel for direction, the pace of swing needed for a given distance, ease of motion rather than forcing the swing, the lovely feel of flush contact, a sense of balance, the realization that one need not help the ball into the air, and the confidence of getting up and down once you are near the green. These are cardinal lessons and requirements for good golf.

When Bob first explained this method to us at *Golf Digest*, it seemed a revelation. It reminded me of the eminent biologist T. H. Huxley's reaction to reading Charles Darwin's *On the Origin of Species*: "How incredibly stupid not to have thought of that myself," he said. Toski's approach is appealing because there's hardly a drop of instruction jargon to confuse you. It takes a degree of patience, to be sure, but like all first-class ideas, it is simple and easy to do.

The idea wasn't particularly new; Englishman Guy Campbell had included a version of it in a book he wrote for beginners in 1922. Years later, Lloyd Mangrum endorsed the idea: "The easiest shot in golf is a one-inch putt, so it's better to learn to crawl before trying to walk or run." Apparently, Harvey Penick had come to the same conclusion and noted it in his then-private little red notebook, which has since been published. If both Penick and Toski thought it was a sound idea, why don't more teachers teach it? Why don't we see this method pushed by the golf magazines and taught on television? I suppose it's because we're in a rush to do most things. And I'm pretty sure the idea wouldn't sell many golf magazines, either.

With due respect to Palmer's comments, it's all very well for Arnold to say that he favors an uncomplicated approach to teaching golf, but when he was learning to bash the ball as a kid, I doubt he would have tolerated Toski's idea, either. And why should he? He was born with superb hand-eye coordination. His dad, Deacon Palmer, very shrewdly found a way to curb his son's youthful aggression and temptations of long hitting (which incidentally the father did not want to discourage) by forcing Arnold into a sound grip. The young Arnie would not have had the patience to learn from the hole out because, like millions of kids, he couldn't wait to smash the ball into the next township. Why should he wait, if he already knew how to hit it? To learn from the hole out, then, is less a temptation than a dare, and I dare say that, if your youngster lacks the kind of talent Palmer had, Toski would dare you and your kid to try it.

One of the things Deacon Palmer (left) taught his son Arnold (right) was the importance of a good grip, something that stood the son in good stead throughout a long, marvelous career.

THE HANDS

One topic that's bound to start an argument among golf gurus is the role of the hands in the swing. Some of the better known of them have said the hands are the source of the most irresistible temptations in a golf swing. A dear friend, Kyle Burton, who has been a fine player and teaching professional for fifty years, insists, with the certainty of the Pope, that the hands must not be used at all in the blessed event. They are along for the ride, he believes, and must not be consciously engaged without inviting the wayward shots and loss of confidence all golfers want to avoid. What stops me whenever we talk is that this fellow is among the longest and straightest drivers I have seen.

A fairly impressive number of gurus agree with Kyle and believe nothing but evil can result from the use of the hands. One is never sure if these gurus mean to include the wrists in their condemnations, but one certainly hopes not because, in that event, the swing would be robbed of all its life. However, these fellows may have a point because a sense of keeping the hands relatively quiet seems to work with certain golfers.

A golf teacher, whose name I can't recall, observed: "The hands are the only part of the human body touching the club." So why ignore them? Most of the masters understood how important the hands are in golf. They might argue about which hand should be dominant, or whether the two should share the load, but not many were willing to disown them altogether.

Gene Sarazen, as practical a golfer as ever was, claimed: "Bad golf is played with the shoulders and the body; good golf is played with the hands. The golfer who aspires to a sound game must remember that the hands are the generals. A correct grip and correct stance lead naturally and easily to a sound swing, and a natural swing is the key to golf without tears."

Sarazen explained that golfers "will discover the swing best suited to themselves, and should resist the blandishments of professionals who want to make them over in their own likeness." Furthermore, he said, a golfer doesn't have to worry about things like cocking the wrists, because "the wrists cock all by themselves." They haven't changed since Sarazen's day.

Gene Sarazen was a great believer in the importance of using the hands in the golf swing. Sarazen's simple swing lasted longer than anyone's but Snead's, and he was the first to win golf's four majors.

Tommy Armour believed that correct hitting involved a lashing action with the right hand. In his view, the left hand was used only as a stabilizer, so to speak. What heresy this seemed! "Hit the ball with the right hand just as hard as you can while keeping the body steady," said Armour. That too was heresy, as most modern theorists—and all top players—move the lower body aggressively during the forward swing. But Armour had an answer: "The faster the hands move, the faster the clubhead will move. Now, if the body is moving ahead, too, the *relative* speed of the hands will be diminished." This almost sounds as if Armour had been reading Einstein. The old notion of hitting against a steady left side and braced left leg, the standard technique from Bob Ferguson to Bob Jones, from Willie Park to Willie Macfarlane, seems a discredited one today, but is there not enough truth in Armour's observation to provoke another look?

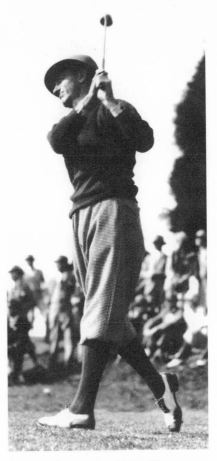

Tommy Armour, a Hall of Famer as both player and teacher, didn't mind golfers using their hands to create speed. He always did, and had an interesting take on the relative speed of hands, body and golf swing.

35

The inventor of the "Vardon" grip was not old Harry but J. L. "Johnny" Laidlay, a Scotsman who won the British Amateur Championship twice in the days of John Ball and Harold Hilton. Laidlay's hands were huge, and so were Vardon's, which a contemporary described as looking like "a bunch of bananas." Sarazen described his friend Tommy Armour's hands as "big as hams, and the envy of us all." Hogan and Nelson both had large hands, so it would appear that this may be an asset in golf and possibly a reason why the Vardon grip has enjoyed such popularity. Big hands are an advantage in the "digital" sports. Sandy Koufax had enormous digits; Michael Jordan's hands are large even for such a big man. Yet, despite the advantages of huge paws, some manage without. Nicklaus and Woods, two of the best players who have ever been, have small hands, and both, incidentally, use the interlocking grip.

Among golf's straightest drivers, history would include Vardon, of course, Wild Bill Mehlhorn, Walter Travis, Byron Nelson, and Orville Moody. Without too much argument, we could also make room on this list for Tommy Armour, Ben Hogan post-1948 and 1949, Lee Trevino, and Annika Sorenstam, who is the straightest in golf today (Jesper Parnevik calls her the female Iron Byron) and, with the aid of modern technology and apologies to Mickey Wright, probably the longest straight driver in the history of women's golf. What did these players say about the use of the right hand? Of both hands? Everyone knows that Hogan struggled for years before solving his swing problems, but that, once he did, Ben was supremely confident he could release his power without fear of hooking. The right hand which had for so long troubled him was now his friend, and Hogan could say with all candor: "When I get to the hitting zone, I wish I had four right hands."

Two of the straightest drivers in history were Orville Moody (left), winner of the U. S. Open in 1969, and Wild Bill Mehlhorn (right), whose golf swing Ben Hogan was said to admire. Sadly, neither man could putt.

As to grip pressure, the orthodox view, including Hogan's, has been that gripping firmly with the last three fingers of the left hand is a desirable feature of any swing, and is particularly useful to avoid hooking. However, John Jacobs disagreed, and offered this explanation: "A combination of a firm left hand and a light right hand, while fine for doing away with slicing, is likely to aggravate hooking," Jacobs said. "The reason is that a tight left-hand grip tends to slow the handle end of the club as it moves into the hitting area, thus allowing the clubhead to lash forward and close the face prematurely. A soft right-hand grip causes the right wrist to be extremely supple and active, so that it too can contribute to the lash." So to stop hooking in particularly incorrigible cases, my own included, John would suggest holding on more firmly with the *right* hand, and it worked because this balanced the forces of the swing more evenly between the two hands and wrists, and this encouraged a more or less square clubface at impact.

Golf literature and the instruction seen on television is full of well-meaning differences of opinion as to which is the "master" side in golf, the right or the left. Harry Vardon was the first man of whom it was whispered that he drove into his own divots from one round to the next. This was a harmless confection later applied to Hogan as well. Vardon believed that golf is a two-sided affair.

"I don't believe in a master hand or master arm," Vardon said. "Playing golf is a two-handed affair, and both should work as one." He paused to point out what really matters: "The one important thing is that the hands, wrists, arms *and clubhead* should be considered part of the club, all working together as one piece of machinery." This is an image echoed many years later by Hogan, of whom it was said that he was a "shaft swinger," rather than a swinger of the hands or the clubhead. In Hogan's swing, it was all of a piece, as it was with Vardon.

Henry Cotton, England's great player of the 1930s and 1940s, believed the hands were the truest motivators in a golf swing. After his career was done, Henry spent much of his time teaching and designing the occasional golf course. "Golf teachers put too much accent on swing, and not enough on finding the ball and strengthening the hands and arms," said Cotton, whose words ring as true today as when he uttered them fifty years ago. Henry would place a huge truck tire on the ground and ask pupils to

Henry Cotton, practicing at St. Andrews in 1933, developed a drill for strengthening the hands by hitting a large tire, which helped build the correct feel for impact; it also helped beginners learn how to use the hands properly when escaping from sand.

whack it with an old five-iron he had nearby. The trick was, you had to hit the tire broadside, not just anywhere on the rubber, and you had to swing the club with speed so it produced a loud pop! When executed correctly by Henry's standards, the pupil had to use equal force with both hands so that both the handle and the head of the club contacted the tire simultaneously. This, said Cotton, developed a sense of striking the tire (and later, the ball) smartly and correctly without holding anything back. Not only was he teaching pupils how to swing the club and hit a golf ball with release, he was instilling in them the feel of using the hands properly in the swing. Though never saying so in so many words, Cotton was also forcing the pupil to follow Hogan's concept of swinging the shaft rather than the hands or the clubhead because only by feeling the entire shaft swinging could the pupil contact the tire squarely. This drill was also used occasionally by several American pros, including Harvey Penick, although he cautioned against swinging so hard that the pupil might hurt a hand or a wrist.

This is not to say that methods advocated by Ernest Jones (swing the clubhead) or Eddie Merrins (swing the handle) are any less to be admired. Either of these ideas may help golfers solve their swing problems. Merrins, the pro at Bel Air in Los Angeles for so many years, is known as The Little Pro, not because of his reputation, which is immense, but his short stature. Not only a fine teacher, Eddie was a first-class player admired for his classic swing and the enviable way he controlled the ball. Merrins wants pupils to feel they are "swinging the handle" on every golf shot, including putts, a technique that gets results under his careful tutelage and also harkens back to Hogan's notion of swinging the shaft.

Long hitting usually tempts everyone, especially amateurs, but to control the ball is the mark of an accomplished golfer. There have probably been players who could match Ken Venturi in his ability to get the ball to follow his will, but few would have surpassed him in his mastery of those lovely little approaches played with anything from a three-quarters swing to a crisp chipping stroke.

"My right hand did everything," Venturi said. "That's the hand I painted all my shots with. I maintain that the left hand has only two functions—to hold on, and not break down." Wouldn't we all like to graft that image onto our own strokes?

THE DELAYED HIT

This may be the place to coin a new axiom: The Delayed Hit is the Delayed Swing which gives us the Deprived Golfer. Other than the advice to keep your head down, it is hard to imagine worse advice to the high-handicap player than that he or she should consciously try to "delay the hit." Here is true controversy, because many pros, even today, teach the virtues of a delayed hit. But careful observation suggests that most golfers fail to use their hands and wrists early enough in the downswing because, frankly, they get lazy or scared of the hit and heave the shoulders before moving the silly club from the top. In fact, you cannot "hit" too early—i.e., use the hands and wrists—if they are traveling on a sound swing path and as long as the lower body is moving in a tempo that supports the swing. Jack Nicklaus, Tommy Armour, John Jacobs, even Bobby Jones have said so in so many words, and if that isn't sufficient authority we are dolts indeed. Yet we continue to hear the virtues of the "delayed hit."

Are these opinions not good enough? Then listen to Joyce Wethered, one of the great female golfers: "Keep the right shoulder back sufficiently long to allow yourself to *feel* that you can swing the clubhead down at the ball inside the line of play." To be fair, Miss Wethered also spoke of the "late hit being a secret to power," but only after the swing has been properly launched, as she described. John Jacobs advised those who tended to lock arms and shoulders together as they start the downswing to feel as though they were "casting from the top, just as a crack angler would do." Jacobs is madly hooked on fly fishing and loved this analogy. Butch Harmon today preaches that golfers would do well to widen the space between forearm and shoulder as fast as possible as the downswing proceeds. Pure Jacobs. Pure Wethered. Pure joy!

Sadly, the delayed hit is among the easiest concepts to describe and illustrate both in golf magazines and books as well as on the teaching tee, and it has a certain ring to it. Unfortunately, it's all quite wrong, especially for the high handicapper and the beginner who may be induced to hold on until there is no chance to make decent contact with the ball—in other words, they delay releasing the club until it's too late to deliver the club smartly and squarely.

Professionals and scratch golfers learn very early in their careers to swing the arms and wrists with speed—and they can do so because they have excellent hand-eye coordination—because they learn that this is the only way to hit far. Their chief problem, also learned early on, lies in curbing their natural instincts and abilities by moving the lower body so that it supports the high speed of their arm swings. Why? Because only in this way can they control their shots. This is why you'll hear good players who are relatively inexperienced as teachers talking a great deal about lower body movements, hips and knees, and all the rest. For them, it's quite true that they needed to move the lower body energetically when refining their swings, but they had already mastered the up-and-down swing action, whose only real power is supplied by the arms and wrists. In any event, the so-called "delayed hit" is an effect, not the cause, of a sound swing, so for any beginner or intermediate golfer it's probably not worth troubling oneself about.

Gardner Dickinson was an assistant to Ben Hogan for a while and spent hours studying Ben's swing. Some felt that Dickinson tried to copy the great man too closely, but Gardner did quite well on the pro tour and had an interesting observation about the dangers of grooving a late hit.

"Hogan exhibited rather a late hit with his old swing of the 1930s and early 1940s, but he had corrected this flaw by the time he won all those majors. I recall a young fellow who had an old picture of Ben just short of impact with the shaft pointing almost straight up. When he met Hogan, he produced the photo and asked Ben where the shot would have gone. 'I have no idea, but I know it wasn't very high,' Hogan replied. Urging golfers to cultivate a late hit is one of the worst pieces of advice I've ever heard. I've never had it explained to my satisfaction why that would make the ball go farther or straighter. I know it will make the ball go lower, and maybe start more to the left, but that's about all this harmful piece of advice will accomplish. The two players in my memory who hit the latest were the worst and wildest drivers I ever saw."

We might clear up one technical point before going on—the hands by themselves supply very little in speed to the hit; only the wrists and arms can do that, as Alistair Cochran and his team of scientists of the Golf Society of Great Britain so clearly and so usefully explained several decades ago. Speed applied correctly, which is to say the clubface meeting the ball squarely at impact, is the secret to obtaining distance in golf. Speed has almost nothing to do with a golfer's size or with the more obvious examples of strength such as big muscles in the back, shoulders, or legs. In almost every era, little fellows like Ian Woosnam, Bob Toski, Ben Hogan, and Chi Chi Rodriguez have been among golf's longest hitters. Each of them had a suppleness and speed of arm and wrist that created terrific force at impact. When they hit the ball squarely, their drives soared past most of their rivals. The message here is that even relatively short or skinny folks can generate plenty of distance if they improve their flexibility and general muscle tone. Look at Charles Howell III, thin and wiry as a whippet and one of the tour's longest hitters. There are, of course, a few other qualities such golfers possess that seem to be especially useful for golf.

THE REQUISITES OF A GOLF SWING

As far as one can tell, very few physical attributes are needed to produce acceptable golf shots. Among them, one might wish for better-than-average endowments of the following: Hand-eye coordination, Balance, Flexibility, and Feel. Other useful physical skills would include: Aiming, Timing, and Space (from the ball), which is related to posture. Let's start with two easy examples: Room To Swing (space) and Aiming.

Room To Swing

Keeping the space between you and the ball more or less constant during the swing is probably as important as all the other so-called fundamentals. It's certainly the least mentioned of the mechanical or physical necessities of a sound, repeating action. Why is this important? Because you want enough space to swing your arms and the club freely past your body, without interference. No blockage, in other words. In his book, *Let 'er Rip*, which every student of the golf swing should own, Gardner Dickinson called this one of the elegant secrets of a sound golf technique: "Do not allow the body to take your swing to a place where you can't get at the ball with your hands at the proper time."

If as you swing through you reduce the space between you and the ball by dipping or crouching, for example, then the arms and club won't have room enough to swing through. Something must give, and it always does. It may be the knees, or an elbow, or the wrists, or the path of the swing, but something will surely give. The distance between you and the ball, both at address and at impact, is related to posture, of course. We should also mention that maintaining the space between player and ball is probably the easiest of the basics to master because there is room for play between the two, so the measurement is not at all fixed. With a little patience, you can certainly work this out for yourself.

When you hear golf pros, especially the teaching pros, talk of maintaining the spine angle during the swing, this is essentially what they're referring to. Keeping the spine angle more or less constant gives the golfer room to swing through without interference. Forty years ago, Paul Runyan pointed to a spot halfway between the neck and left shoulder, identifying the mysterious spot as the "suspension point." A line drawn from suspension point to ball must never crumble or fold, Runyan preached. He too was giving the pupil "room to swing."

Bob MacDonald, a native of Dornoch, was a friend and frequent companion of Walter Hagen's. MacDonald came to America, and after a year or so in Buffalo, settled in Chicago, where he became a famous teacher in the 1920s and 1930s. When Babe Didrickson took up golf in earnest, she came to Chicago for sessions with MacDonald, who had the same idea as Runyan. MacDonald described the center of the swing as being in the left shoulder joint so pupils could sense the space that would allow them to easily release the swinging club. Other teachers have found their own ways to explain this very useful principle of golf. If you want graphic examples, watch films of Walter Hagen and Sam Snead, to cite two quite different styles, measuring themselves from the ball just before they start their swings. With them, it seemed almost instinctive.

Of course, the great players—and anyone who makes it to the pro tour is in that company—learn this fundamental at their mother's knee, or, if they don't, have the blessed gift of hand-eye coordination that allows them to compensate by a quick thrust of the trunk or a slap of the wrist or some such unnecessary lurch or flourish in the forward swing. You may not be able to see this in many cases, as their swings tend to move faster than the eye can follow. However, you can often see the after-effects by watching the finish of a golfer's swing.

Aiming

In aiming, as in alignment, golfers can try to be too precise. The best results are apt to come when you get a sense of the thing rather than trying to measure it with a laser. The human body isn't built to react to laser measurements. On the other hand, the body is a stunningly able mechanism. It can process more information in a heartbeat than any computer, and can react faster and more accurately. Maybe not for launching missiles, but very nicely for launching golf balls with our gaudy, modern implements.

When it comes to aiming, we can turn to another of Harvey Penick's observations. Rather than aim first and then hit, try hitting shots until you achieve solid contact. "You are aiming where the ball goes on solid contact," Penick said. If his comment is not explicit enough, here is how Harvey explained it:

"Don't worry about where you're aiming. Ignore that for the moment and simply hit shots with a full swing until you make solid contact. When you do, notice where the ball goes. That's where you're aiming, son."

Harvey had figured out that noticing where the ball goes, and how it is shaped in flight, are sovereign principles of golf. And he knew so well that it's not worth noticing until you can hit the ball reasonably flush. That's something that many crack golfers learn instinctively as young boys and girls. Many modern teachers advise golfers to "see the target" before you swing and visualize the shot as you swing. There is nothing wrong with this advice, as the mind tends

It took a genius like Harvey Penick to simplify such a complicated business as learning how to aim your shots. Harvey works with a pupil at his favorite haunt, the Austin Country Club.

to govern the body in these matters, but there are other influences at work once we step onto the golf course. Trees. Lakes. Bunkers. Swamps. Weeds and bushes. Angry insects. Gusts of wind. That sort of thing. Ignore these distractions if you will, but most of us cannot. What happens then? We try too hard to aim the shot, to steer the ball into safe pastures, and this usually makes us restrict our golf swing.

Another Texas guru, Jack Burke Jr., presides over a tree-lined golf paradise in Houston where aiming is a particularly necessary part of the game. To those intimidated by tight fairways, Burke poses a question:

"Ever notice what happens when you get to a hole with a high tee and a wide open fairway? You get an immediate sense of freedom. You feel as though you can hit it 'anywhere,' but you don't. Usually, the ball goes far and straight. Why? Because you're not trying to steer it,

Jack Burke Jr. won the Masters and the PGA and many other tournaments because he had the gift. He also had learned a few helpful tricks, like allowing himself to swing freely, even recklessly to encourage both distance and direction.

so your swing moves freely." So when you come to those holes with obstacles and tight fairways, use your imagination constructively.

"Imagine you're aiming a shot at the ocean," Burke said. "It doesn't matter where the ball goes. Just let it all go. Swing free and easy." Easy for him to say, but true enough.

Burke's admonition homes in on one of the great secrets in golf, alluded to earlier. The brain knows where you want to hit the ball and the body will respond pretty much automatically in its dumb desire to achieve the brain's goal—as long as you don't interfere. You can interfere in a hundred ways—by blocking the hips, by swinging so hard that the arms move the club out of plane or path, by reducing the space between yourself and the ball thus not allowing room to swing freely, by imagining evil consequences, and in many other ways. Far better that you should give the brain a chance to let the body work, in aiming as in so many other aspects of the game. This is not so easy when you have an opponent (or he has you) on the ropes at the last and all you need is a good drive and a solid second. But that's golf.

We have touched on two of the seven deadly sins (call them temptations) of lust (for power) and greed (which seems rather closely aligned with its partner), but we've barely mentioned those of pride, envy, anger, and sloth. Those will be dealt with one way or another in the next few chapters. I will assume that the ones of sneakiness (kicking a ball in the rough) and lying (about one's score) would not be tolerated by anyone honorable and clever enough to buy and read this book. Or you may wish to ignore all of this and follow the example of Willie Nelson, another Texas boy who treats temptation with the contempt (or is it the respect?) it deserves. Nelson became hooked on golf and sometimes prefers it to picking on his battered old guitar—into which, as country and western fans know, he has scratched a permanent, raggedy old hole. Nelson bought a golf course outside Austin, Texas, and has his own raggedy set of rules. "Par is anything I want it to be," Willie told a visitor, pointing to a fairway wandering off in front of them. "This hole right here, for example, is a par-forty-seven, and yesterday I birdied the sucker."

CHAPTER
THREE

THE MYTHS OF GENIUS

---

*"It is time these gentlemen were finding out that eccentricities
of instinct are only the evidences of genius, not the creators of it."*
—Mark Twain

The recognition and appreciation of genius is a delightful experience for all of us and leads to all sorts of muddle and myth. Golfers rejoice to watch the genius of Ben Hogan and Sam Snead, of Arnold Palmer and Jack Nicklaus, of Raymond Floyd and Lee Trevino, and of Tiger Woods. If there are common swing elements to be found in this crowd, I defy you to name them. In neither grips, stances, postures, swing planes, nor tempos were any of these fellows alike. They did, in fact, follow certain fundamentals, to borrow a somewhat misunderstood and suspect term, but had no choice in the physical principles of club meeting ball correctly because those are the same for everyone, whether your name is Nicklaus or Noodlemeyer.

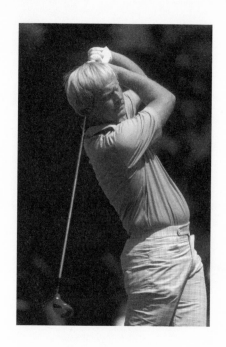

The great ones' swings don't look alike, and neither do ours. Would Jack Nicklaus (right) use Trevino's grip? or Tiger Woods use Jim Furyk's (center) backswing? or Raymond Floyd (far right) use Palmer's posture? Each golfer follows his own idiosyncracies.

If Hogan and Snead both learned to play their best golf with a slightly open clubface, would we say that Palmer and Trevino were wrong to prefer a closed one? One may have an opinion about this, but one can draw no clear, simple conclusions other than to say that each of these players concocted a method that worked for him, and only him. Let Nicklaus play with Trevino's grip and swing plane and see if he might ever have escaped from the pleasant fields of Scioto. Let Floyd try the Palmer posture and see how great a genius he would be in the short game. Let Woods try Furyk's backswing and, well, you get the idea.

There is an odd and rather unfortunate habit in golf instruction of describing the idiosyncrasies of swing of one player or another as an example or proof of a fundamental principle when in fact the idiosyncrasy is peculiar to that given player and is, as Twain might say, the evidence rather than the cause of his genius. Lee

Trevino, one of the great ball strikers, has a swing one would not recommend to others. Few swings are more admired than those of Bobby Jones and Sam Snead, yet the swing actions of both men came, as the phrase goes, slightly "over the top" (although nearly always on the true line), a method that one would not commend to the average golfer either, primarily because of the exquisite timing such an action requires, but both men possessed almost perfectly.

Putting this business more bluntly, to apply Ben Hogan's theories to the multitudes might well destroy them. While there is a great deal to admire in Hogan's book, *Five Lessons: The Modern Fundamentals of Golf*, and in his subsequent revelations, Paul Runyan and later swing experts pointed out that these are really nothing more than a defense against hook, and a rather bad one at that. They suggested that to prescribe Hogan's fundamentals or to graft his "cures" indiscriminately onto the majority of weekend golfers would probably lead to more harm than good. Hogan said as much himself in his article in *Life* that revealed his "secret"—a cupping of the left wrist at the top of the backswing. "I doubt this will be worth a doggone to the weekend duffer, and it will ruin a bad golfer," Ben wrote. Imagine a publisher today letting Tiger Woods or Ernie Els get away with such candor.

Ben Hogan's legendary work ethic and astonishing recovery from a horrible car crash are an inspiration to every golfer. Certainly they were to Steve Jones, who was inspired by Hogan's story when Steve won the 1996 U. S. Open. But the plain truth is that we can no more copy the genius of others than leap into their skins. Did Hogan copy Snead? Did Horowitz emulate Rubenstein? Impossible. In each man, the expression of his genius was entirely his own, as it must be for each of us.

"The masters play as it suits them to play, and then evolve theories to explain why the particular movements they discover themselves using are right," Percy Boomer observed. Boomer grew up in the English Channel island of Jersey where Harry Vardon and his brothers learned their golf, and became an influential teacher in the first half of the twentieth century. Boomer continued:

"Unfortunately, a shot that may work in the hands of a master may have disastrous results if copied by a less expert player." Later he added: "We all start off teaching by pointing out a pupil's faults, then curing them according to a formula we favor. I did this for twenty-five years before discovering that the best way to get pupils to hit the ball satisfactorily is to watch for any good, natural qualities that may be there, and then build up a swing around them." For example, instead of telling a pupil he was over-swinging and breaking his left arm (an example of negative teaching), Boomer would explain the positive benefits of adding width in the swing while leaving the pupil free to use his or her natural swing tendencies.

When Bob Toski came on tour in 1948 he was a raw sliver of gristle and bone with a pair of hands that allowed him to do almost anything he wanted with his golf swing. This kind of talent can be a blessing or a curse. Ben Hogan was the hero of the hour, so like most young guys Toski began to practice some of Hogan's swing mannerisms.

"I used to watch Ben by the hour," Toski said. "I thought if Hogan can do it, so can I."

The two men were about the same size, so why not? One day as Toski was working diligently on the practice tee, Sam Snead walked by and stopped for a moment to watch.

"Mouse," he drawled, "what the hell are you doing?" Toski said he was working on his swing. "Well, you're swinging awful," said Snead. Toski explained that he was trying to emulate some of the moves Hogan made.

Snead glared at Toski, put his hand on the little man's shoulder and said: "You don't need to swing like Hogan. You don't need to swing like Snead, either. You need to swing like Toski. You've got one hell of a golf swing, and I don't want to see you swinging like that anymore." Snead turned to leave, then came back: "The good Lord didn't give you the body of Ben Hogan or Sam Snead; he gave you the body of Bob Toski. It's not very big, but if you're good enough, you're big enough! Now, you go back to swinging like you know how, and I'll be back in a while to check on you."

Sam Snead (in straw hat) kept an eye on Bob Toski (swinging, foreground) on the practice tee and offered the smaller man a valuable lesson in golf—swing like Toski, not Hogan or Snead, and you'll play your best.

Half an hour later, Snead returned and found Toski using his own natural swing action and nailing every shot. "That's Bob Toski," Snead growled. "You play like Toski, and you'll be successful." And so he did. Bob would remember Snead's advice about "good enough, big enough" for the better part of a lifetime, and pass it along to others.

We are all, nevertheless, after golf's holy grail and the devil take anyone who stands in our way. Not one of us believes we are beyond help or more than an inside tip away from genius, and if we think we can learn "the secret" from David Leadbetter or from reading the comments of Tiger Woods in a magazine, we will surely seek our salvation there. Golfers tend to believe in the tooth fairy and half expect a genie to appear one day to touch us on the shoulder and cure us of our golfing ills.

If you had a dream and you could pick the greatest player, the finest shotmaker who ever lived to be your private tutor for a day, who would you pick? Jack Nicklaus? Ben Hogan? Bobby Jones? Byron Nelson? Tiger Woods? Sam Snead? A large number would pick Ben Hogan, no doubt because of his reputation as a brilliant analyst and eventual master of his own swing. Hogan had little patience with teaching others, even gifted players. Yet a few men and one or two women—Gardner Dickinson, John Schlee, Mark O'Meara, Kris Tschetter—actually persuaded Hogan to coach them. Dickinson and Schlee soaked up Hogan's every word and move, but not O'Meara. Mark used Hogan clubs, so when he turned pro he wrote to Ben asking for help with his swing. Hogan surprisingly agreed to watch him hit shots and offer what advice he could. Off they went to Shady Oaks, Hogan's private club in Fort Worth, and headed for the practice ground where O'Meara began hitting balls.

"I was hitting it great," he recalls. "Mr. Hogan told me things about my swing and changed my setup a little bit. I started hitting it worse, and asked him what he thought."

"That looks a lot better," Hogan said.

O'Meara thought to himself: "I'm not going to do this. I'm better off with what I've got." He returned to his old ways, and ignored the advice Hogan offered, perhaps the only recorded instance in which someone has turned a cold shoulder to the secret swing lore of Ben Hogan.

THE UNFORTUNATE IMPERATIVES

Let us suppose for a moment that more than a little of what's been written about the art of swinging a golf club is rubbish. History teaches us that humankind is desperate for salvation and is most easily drawn to the quickest and cheapest kind. Enter the golf instruction magazine and its wily offspring, the how-to book. Some of these books and articles claim to reveal a secret, or even "The" secret. If only it were true. It is in the nature of golf that no one will quite master it, a condition it shares with life. A few men have come close, however, although the most brilliant strikers among these—Vardon, Jones, Hogan, Snead, Trevino—have seemed the least willing to prescribe a method or a secret. Hogan's "secret" was advertised by a publisher, not by Hogan himself. He chuckled, in fact, while collecting the $50,000 fee. Vardon and Jones each wrote extensively and brilliantly on golf, although Vardon had help and Jones didn't need it, and what strikes the reader most about their books is how little dogma colored their views. In conversation, both Snead and Hogan were more sensible and wiser than anything in their books (one might add to this list John Ball, Jimmy Demaret, and Peter Thomson, figures of lesser light but equally wise in their understanding of the game and reticence in prescribing a method).

Which brings us to those common injunctions I'm always tempted to call "the unfortunate imperatives," unfortunate because they are misleading, and by misleading I mean that they often can lead to harm. Golfers will recognize these imperatives immediately because they are preceded by words like "must" or "should" or "must not" or, best of all, "never." When you hear or read one of these giddy imperatives, embrace it with the same enthusiasm you would a tarantula. The reason is plain enough, because so many of these well-meant admonitions can lead to a nest of troubles. Ignore them. If you possess no spark of genius, then no amount of drills, setting of angles, keeping heads down (dreadful advice) or high finishes will improve your lot. Better that you should learn to putt and chip, which almost every member of the human race can learn to do, and be content with your limitations in the long game. So it's all right to be suspicious of instruction books that use terms like "must" and "always." If you come upon a sentence like "you must never do such-and- such," you can assume that the author probably means well, but is trying too hard to convince.

It should be clear from this that I'm with those who view golf as an entirely individual enterprise. Each of us learns differently because our physical coordination and instincts are our own. When we see golf swings as different as Raymond Floyd's, Eamon Darcy's, Gene Littler's, John Daly's, Jim Furyk's, and David Duval's, we can reasonably conclude that style or even mechanical uniformity are not terribly important. There is the old canard about "all the great players look the same at impact." To this one might be tempted to respond, "Yeah, and how many of those guys started the swing at impact?"

The point is that the forces that shape impact and the flight of the ball are developed idiosyncratically by each individual, by his or her setup to the ball and by the movements in the backswing and the downswing. Sergio Garcia is among the latest geniuses— and he may prove to be one of the best ever—but how many of us would survive using his method? His flattish plane, the decided layoff of the club at the top of the swing, and the brutal downcock in the downswing would send most of us to the nearest physical

How many of us would survive trying to swing like Sergio Garcia? The Spaniard does just fine with his violent contortions, but we mortals might wind up at the physical therapist's. A uniform style is not required, nor even desirable in golf.

therapist and our golf shots darting into the nearest rabbit hole. But can anyone doubt his talent or his game?

Not everyone would agree with the conclusions I've listed below, but I'll offer a few general suggestions that might help beginning golfers.

• It's a good idea to hold on to the club as you swing it. This seems fairly obvious, although you don't have to hold on with both hands all the way through the swing. Too many one-armed golfers have learned to play quite successfully, and too many fellows—Bobby Jones and Lee Trevino, for two—let go of the club and re-gripped it at some point during the swing.

• The movement of the body is less important than the action of the arms and wrists. Try hitting a shot with your arms strapped to your sides and the body free, and then another with the arms free and the body restricted (for example, while sitting in a chair). Which shot went farther?

• Hitting the back of the ball will usually produce straighter and longer shots. As we learn in golf, this is not always true (for example, when the clubface is open or closed at impact), but it's worth keeping in mind for most basic shots.

• Try to keep the body in balance during the swing, much as you would in dancing. Gary Player, for one, seemed to violate this suggestion on so many of his shots, but he has a superb sense of balance and manages to get away with it. Hogan and Snead were both good dancers. The feet and legs are the principal actors in this game of good balance, as they are in all sports.

• Leave enough space between you and the ball so that you can swing through without any blockage or encumbrance. This is

Welshman Ian Woosnam is a golfer who leaves plenty of room between himself and the ball, which lets him release his swing without fuss. The result is that he's a long hitter who gets maximum distance and, incidentally, hits straighter shots.

why good players measure themselves in the act of addressing the ball to be sure that there is enough room for arms and club to pass the body freely. Watch films of Sam Snead or Ian Woosnam, and the easy freedom so apparent in the swing of Annika Sorenstam. No crouching or dipping or lunging needed by those players.

Freedom of motion is so apparent in the finish of Annika Sorenstam's golf swing, a secret to the great distance she obtains.

WHAT ABOUT CONSISTENCY?

For every such disclaimer, there are probably ten golf teachers who will say, with some justification: "That's all very well, but we are after consistency, and you can hardly be consistent if you don't, for example, hold on to the club during the swing." Really? Then how do we explain Bobby Jones, who let loose of the club on virtually every full swing? Vijay Singh does the same at impact. Bob Toski has pointed out that Jones also had a rather loose, distinctly bent left arm at address which continued through much of the backswing, but it straightened as the downswing progressed and was firm as a rod at impact and then folded as the right arm straightened in the follow-through. This is all a bit technical, but fairly typical of a golf swing that lasts. It may also be another clue that in the great ones, things happen by instinct. Jones didn't need to know that he must straighten his left arm at impact; it happened automatically because his body knew it. Our bodies, it turns out, know more than we do. When Harvey Penick told his students, "Trust your swing," this is what the old master was getting at.

This process of the body knowing things doesn't happen only in the golf swings of the great ones; it happens in our swings, too. The trick for us, I think, is to *allow* it to happen rather than contrive something that may or may not work. We know that what the mind sets as the task the body will try to do. We also know that the mind cannot be fooled by the body. For example, if we swing on a path that travels from out to in, the mind sees that the

Vijay Singh loses the grip with his right hand during impact, a peculiarity of his method that probably happens more frequently than he would like, yet he is still one of the longest, straightest hitters in golf.

ball will most certainly go left without some form of correction, so it instructs the hands to open the clubface in compensation. The result is golf's commonplace, the pulled slice in which the ball starts out to the left and then curves back to the right. Or in another example, if we are perhaps crouched too far over the ball as we swing, the mind knows to tell the legs and feet to stand on tiptoe so as to allow the arms and club enough room to pass through. As the mind sees it, this is only common sense, and it needn't bother us with such trifling details.

Golf does not lend itself to too careful analysis. It is more mental and emotional than mechanical; it is more reactive than active, and thus instinctive. Trying to force body parts into particular "ideal" positions robs a golfer of his or her natural freedom of movement. "There's a certain recklessness in good golf," observes Jack Burke Jr., one of canniest and most respected of golf's masters. Watch Chad Campbell, one of the newer stars on tour, who cracks the ball with that wonderful, reckless sense of release. It is useful for golfers to understand the physics of golf, but most attempts to explain the game in mechanical terms are quite limiting and, in the end, unsatisfactory. The reason for this, it seems to me, is obvious. As in most things we do, golf is easier learned than taught; put the other way around, one cannot teach golf nearly as well as another can learn it. Loading the mind with ten "musts" and five "nevers" is an invitation to frustration and failure because they paralyze natural movement. If golfers need anything in their games, it is natural movement—the freer, the better. Burke's logic and summons to recklessness is almost reassuring.

Something similar happens with musicians, at least Chopin thought so. The nineteenth century Polish composer and piano virtuoso was a master teacher, too, and a stickler for technique.

Yet he reportedly urged his pupils: "Be bolder, let yourself go," and cautioned against endless practice without cultivating a sympathetic touch, adding: "The only point of technique is freedom."

Harvey Penick and John Jacobs understood such things, although not before years of struggle. Their minds were resilient enough to cast aside idle thoughts, to remove faulty or complicated concepts without fear and replace them with simpler, more useful cures. Most teachers do the same over the course of time, but those two were shrewd enough to see the natural causes and wise enough to accept the instinctive reactions of human nature. It's interesting, too, that each in his own way learned to simplify his message, choosing language and images an average golfer can easily grasp. This is among the handiest, most useful arts of teaching.

John Jacobs would often tell pupils that the golf swing is just "two turns and a swish." By this he meant that we turn away from the ball as we swing the club up, then turn back through as we swing the club down to the ball, and as we do, we want the club to "swish." If we don't interfere with ourselves, that should be enough to carry the club nicely up and around to the finish. Our golf swings are not more complicated than this, Jacobs says, but try not to leave out the "swish"—and try to remember that second turn, the one that moves the left hip out of the way as you swing through. This is shameless oversimplification, but sometimes we need simple images. Harvey Penick never wanted golfers to be too particular about the way they hold the club. Harvey wanted them to find out for themselves if they had a good grip. He would tee up three balls and ask students to hit three shots in a row without taking their hands off the club, or moving their fingers, either. The golfer would find out in a hurry where the shots were going.

John Jacobs, shown here coaching Jose Maria Olazabal, kept instruction simple. Turn back as you pop the club into the correct position at the top and turn through as you swing down and through, Jacobs would say to beginners and great players alike.

"If you can do that without changing your hold on the club, you have a solid grip, and you won't have to worry about that part of your game," Harvey said. No danger of being over-taught by fellows like this.

Following Your Better Instincts

A story is told about Jim Furyk, the fellow with the washing-machine swing and the golden putting touch. His father, Mike Furyk, a club pro, had every opportunity to change his son's swing at an early age. He didn't because he believed his son was following his natural instincts. These were plenty good enough to make him a star athlete in high school, and Mike Furyk knew all about fellows named Miller Barber, Gay Brewer, and Raymond Floyd who succeeded with unorthodox golf swings. When a college golf coach showed up to recruit young Furyk, he told the father that he couldn't wait to get Jim to college so he could change his swing. "Coach, he won't be going to your school," Mike said. As he later reminded the readers of *Golf Digest*, all his son had done so far was win ten million dollars on the pro tour and finish in the top ten in eight majors championships. He's done even better since.

Doug Ford is another whose game was so much more than his swing. When Ford turned pro, Cary Middlecoff said, "I thought that's the biggest waste of money and ambition ever, but he was tough as a nickel steak." Ford had a short, flat, caddie-yard swing that kept his shots in view, which allowed him to control the game and befuddle his opponents. He was one of those players who would look for a weakness in the enemy and find a way to beat him, any way that was legal. Hitting long irons or woods

Most of the pros could outdrive Doug Ford, but not many could outplay him. He was a mainstay of the tour for decades using a tough mind and one of the greatest short games the pros had witnessed.

from the fairways didn't seem to bother Ford, and meanwhile, he would hole everything in sight. He became the modern-day incarnation of the phrase, "He can get it up and down from ball washers." For more than twenty-five years, Doug Ford was among the pro tour's big guns, winning two majors and about twenty tournaments. "Almost everyone could outdrive him, but he'd hit his second before you could blink, then fuss and stare at you while you hit yours. He was a fast player, all right, but with that short game of his, he could score with just about anyone," Middlecoff said. Jerry Barber, one of the all-time short-game wizards, said: "The greatest short game player I have ever seen is Doug Ford. I've played more rounds with Ford than most guys, and I have paid dearly to see it."

His great, natural successor was Seve Ballesteros, an adventurer whose drives were much longer than Ford's, but one whose loose swings often got him in trouble. Seve's spark of genius was in that short game of his, which time and again allowed him to escape the abyss. We would watch him stride to the green with an infectious grin that seemed to say, "There, I did it again." So he did, winning five major championships with a particular talent and competitive drive that carried him to the very top of professional golf. He had a gift, said Jack Whitaker, "of finding a light in the midst of darkness." Seve's countryman Jose Maria Olazabal turned out to be every bit his equal in that dangerous country.

Another wizard crept out of the darkness not long ago. The most remarkable player to emerge in the 1990s was not Tiger Woods or Phil Mickelson, but Allen Doyle, who has done to the Senior Tour (now optimistically renamed the Champions Tour) what Doug Ford did to the big tour. Doyle played a little golf in school, but made his collegiate mark in ice hockey at Norwich University in Vermont. Though his golf swing looks more like Bobby Orr than Bobby Jones, he manages it quite well, and his combative instincts come straight off the ice. He's not bad in the short game, either. Doyle was a good enough and competitive enough

After missing out on the PGA Tour, Allen Doyle crept out of the darkness with an unusual swing and peculiar putting stroke to collect serious money and popular acclaim on the Champions Tour.

golfer to make a couple of Walker Cup teams, but for two decades he remained an obscure amateur. He moved to Georgia and opened a driving range.

When he could, Allen played in and even won a few amateur events. In 1992 Doyle reached the semifinals of the U. S. Amateur, where he lost to Justin Leonard. When the calendar allowed him to try the Senior Tour, he began to win serious money. Soon he was beating the senior stars until they hurt. No one could figure out how this guy managed to finish high in just about every tournament he entered, but he did. Players like Doyle and Ford remind us of the bumblebee who is unaware that he isn't built to fly but flies anyway. These guys break about twenty rules of orthodoxy with their golf swings, yet care bloody less and regularly beat their opponents to their wallets and handsome shares of the prize money. What did Doyle say about this? "I like playing in the shadows," he murmured.

This preference for shady places didn't last. In 2001 Doyle buried a thirty-footer on the last hole and beat Hale Irwin and Doug Tewell for the Senior Players' Championship. That year he led the Senior Tour money list with $2.5 million. Through 2003, he had won about seven million dollars on the creaky tour, and every time you turned on the tube he was quietly finishing in the top five or ten. His swing doesn't go back much higher than his hip pocket, and it's pretty much a blur from there. Players will tell you that his putting stroke has no backswing at all; actually, it may move as much as an inch behind the ball before he strokes it. Well, the ball doesn't notice what Allen does, but it does fall into the hole a lot. Just watching him play makes you wonder about fancy swing theories and all that technical mumbo jumbo. Doyle makes do with what he has, one of those fellows the old curmudgeon Samuel Johnson may have had in mind when he said: "He has very few hooks, but what hooks he has, he uses well."

In case anyone might miss the point, Allen Doyle and Tiger Woods were the top scramblers in pro golf. One year, Allen missed over five hundred greens, but he got up and down on 350 of them, a 68.6 percentage, according to the PGA Tour; Tiger's percentage that year was 69.8. His rivals notice Doyle's mental game more than these trappings, however. He has a strong will and seems to play with a defenseman's notion of "bad intentions." Said Jim Colbert, whose career was built on grit: "When Allen Doyle gets mad, he just gets better. And he does get mad." Like all the great players—Jones, Sarazen, Hogan, Palmer—Doyle has that most valuable ability to turn anger to his own advantage.

There is so little myth to that brand of genius that we might as well take a lesson from it.

The truth is, however, that even if we could play the short game like Doyle or Ballesteros we would all wish to swing like Snead or Woods or Els and we'll search for the grail as long as the game endures. The lure of grand myths is strong in our genes.

Instead, we ought to pay attention to the Doug Fords, the Jerry Barbers, the Allen Doyles, those fellows with the nothing golf swings and the killer instincts who absolutely thrive on beating the big boys. If we could learn to hit fairways or get it up and down in two from 130 yards, as they do, maybe we could beat some of the big boys around our own club. Lloyd Mangrum, the hard-boiled Texan and a Hall

Plenty of his rivals could hit the ball farther and some straighter, and a handful could putt better than Lloyd Mangrum, but he didn't think many could play like he could.

of Famer, won thirty-six times on the pro tour because he understood that his judgment and his nerve were better than his swing. He once told the author Charles Price: "There must be a hundred guys out here who can hit the ball farther than me, and fifty who can hit it straighter. Maybe five can putt better; but they can't *play* like I can."

In the era between Mangrum and Nicklaus, any list of the best players would include Mickey Wright. Some believe she had been the greatest woman player of all, while others simply include her on any list of golf's masters, man or woman. She was very long and straight, an accurate iron player, and she could putt. Mickey Wright could also think with the best of them, which may account for the eighty-two tournaments she won during a Hall of Fame career. Wright won thirteen events in 1963. Only Byron

Mickey Wright's golf swing was as good as you could find, but she claimed her greatest asset was an ability to concentrate and not be distracted. Many believe her to be the greatest woman player in history.

Nelson won more in a single year. "She could have won another hundred tournaments if she hadn't quit early," said Kathy Whitworth, her great contemporary. Mickey Wright retired at age thirty-four. Asked to compare her game to that of the current superstar, Annika Sorenstam, Wright told *Palm Beach Post* writer Craig Dolch: "The similarities are her ability to concentrate and not be distracted, to stay in the moment. It sounds so easy, but it's so hard to do." Not be distracted? Her implication seems to be that there's nothing wrong with all that mechanical stuff, but this is where winning golf comes from. Yes, I know, so easy to say, and so hard to do.

It may cheer struggling golfers to know that the player besides Mickey Wright and Byron Nelson who came closest to mastering the game employed one of the least admired methods. The swing mechanics of Jack Nicklaus were not bad by any means, mind you, but they are seldom held up as an ideal. They were fine for Jack, who had a stocky, powerful body and fabulous hand-eye coordination, but might have destroyed lesser men tempted to copy him. Yet his record until now has eclipsed all others. Jack's power—in his early twenties the equal of Tiger Woods's, as those who saw it can attest—was a great asset, but surely his dominance was due to his intelligence, his will, his control of himself, his superhuman patience, and, not least, his putting.

LEVELS OF THE GAME

Top professional golfers, including both Nicklaus and Woods, spend lots of time practicing mechanics, but they are geniuses to begin with and already possess a champion's intelligence, will, heart, and nose for scoring. There's a message here for all golfers:

Mechanical things have less to do with golf than we might want to believe. Those who spend the greatest part of their time trying to master the physical side of the game tend to miss out the more important bits—determination, discipline, patience, concentration, attitude, strategic thinking, imagination, composure, nerve, desire, and a healthy dose of common sense. Though tempted to include practice among these, I can't for the very good reason that too many grand players have succeeded with very little of it.

Beyond these are the more subtle levels of the game, like the willingness to put one's self forward and seize the winning position, the capacity to shrug aside failure and go on, the strength to rise above doubts, the majestic urge to keep trying, and, at the end, an implacable killer instinct. Beyond these lie higher levels still, those of serenity and confidence, and beyond those the mystical fusion of method and will with the elements. And finally there is resignation.

Many years ago, a match took place that illustrates why golfers should never give up. Bobby Cruickshank met Al Watrous in the first round of the 1932 PGA Championship at Keller Golf Club, in St. Paul, Minnesota. A member of two Ryder Cup teams, Watrous had all but beaten Bobby Jones in the 1926 British Open, only to falter at the seventeenth hole after Jones played one of his miracle shots. Cruickshank was a mighty mite at five-feet-four, a Scot who had settled in America, and he, too, had pushed Jones to the limit in the 1923 U. S. Open at Inwood, New York. Against Wee Bobby at Keller, Watrous built a lead of nine holes with twelve to play; surely the match was over. On the next hole, Watrous generously conceded Cruickshank's five-foot putt for a half. Now Bobby was nine down with eleven to play.

"Poor Al Watrous!" chuckled Paul Runyan, a contemporary and twice PGA champion, who always delighted in relating the story. "On the next eleven holes, Watrous made seven pars, three bogeys, and a birdie, and lost all but two, including the eighteenth, where his birdie kept the match all square. On the fifth extra hole, the forty-first of the match, Cruickshank won when Watrous missed a three-foot putt."

Bobby Cruickshank stood 5-feet-4 and was a dynamo player during the 1920s and 1930s. He played a stunning match in the 1932 PGA Championship that demonstrates why golfers should never give up.

Bobby didn't win the tournament, Olin Dutra did, but the tiny Scot had probably shot his bolt. The incident remains a stunning reminder that the only safe lead in golf is when you're clutching the trophy in your hands. You wouldn't think the emotions play such a big role in golf, but that's another myth the game will shatter.

As for the physical side of the game, there is not much to say. The mechanics of golf can be covered in five short sentences:

1. Hold the club in a way that gives the best chance to allow square contact.

2. Give yourself room to swing.

3. Take the club away with a sense of ease.

4. Do the best you can to swing in balance.

5. Take a tiny bit of Mother Earth as you strike the ball.

Of these, balance is probably the hardest to control and the first to go wrong. Our bodies and moods change from day to day. Ernie Vossler, a top teacher of both pros and amateurs before he went into golf course development, explained: "Balance is a reaction, not an action. It starts with footwork." Ken Venturi said he's seen more swings ruined by mistakes from the waist down—i.e., spinning the hips, too active legs, and poor footwork —than from the upper body.

Seymour Dunn, the Scottish-American teacher, offered this analysis: "The golf swing should be built from the feet up through the body to the hands, like a house, from the foundation up." He added: "Stand on your bones to avoid muscular tenseness and to enable you to brace yourself against the pull of centrifugal force generated when you swing the club." Another old-timer, H. J. Whigham, had a similar idea in 1897. "A golfer will gradually find his swing lengthening out without any conscious effort on his part. If one can learn a true half swing, one is on the road to grace."

Players with relatively fast swing tempos like Hogan, Venturi, Nick Price, and Greg Norman, tend to get very active in their legs. However, Gardner Dickinson pointed out that Hogan's legs moved so slowly during a full swing that he could read a note pinned to Ben's knee. Tommy Bolt was the same, leading us to suppose that in most good players the legs move at a relatively leisurely pace, and never violently. A relatively calm action from the waist down has a lot to do with fixing the rhythm and tempo of the swing, which usually encourages good balance.

Jack Burke Jr. agreed: "In the golf swing, your legs move slowly, probably slower than any other part of your body. You can't have a swing that moves so quickly that it moves past your legs. Timing is set by the legs and feet. Accuracy comes from how well your two knees move along the target line. You can swing only as well as you are coordinated with the lower part of your body. Golfers need to realize what balance and timing skills they have, then learn and be taught the way they're balanced."

It is helpful to know that the arms and wrists supply almost all of the power in a golf swing, that the lower body, as we've just seen, moves in support of the swing, and that the hands, being the only part of you that touches the club, are useful in controlling the shape of your golf shots. All the rest is individual preference. All that is wanted is the good sense to allow one's natural reactions to occur and to swing in a way that offers the least resistance to these entirely personal and natural reactions. Thinking too much about where the knees, elbows, toes, and hips are positioned at various points during the swing is probably more distraction than help.

This is not to say that swing instruction is not useful. It is, when dispensed by a wise teacher. Such persons are apt to couch their tuition in suggestions and images. Once having grasped the idea, the mind will instruct the body quite nicely. Harvey Penick understood this so well. His diagnosis and explanation of aiming, discussed in Chapter Two, is a sweet example of the simplicity at the heart of a complex optical and geometrical business. Most of the physical side of golf is like this. Perhaps it will take a bit of time and practice to find your place, to sense the improvement that brings confidence, but that seems a small price. Those beginners who have neither the time nor the patience are not likely to understand or enjoy the game.

BALL FLIGHT LAWS

Another great help is to understand the physical laws that govern the flight of a golf ball. There are only a few and they're quite easy to grasp. These laws are friendly laws because they are immutable: They are the same for everyone whether your name is Hufnagle or Hogan. Once learned, they are great tools to understanding why we take certain actions playing a shot. Nothing in these laws has anything to do with how the body moves. It helps to remember that the club is the only object that's allowed to touch the ball.

The so-called "Ball-Flight Laws" are nature's own; they are based in physics, and cannot be revoked. They have been observed since about the time golf began, and were fully organized into simple language by Englishman John Jacobs in the 1950s. It is a mark of Jacobs's influence on the modern game that these ball flight laws of his have been incorporated into the teaching programs of most of today's top teachers. They describe what happens at impact to influence ball flight. Here they are:

1. Swing path determines the direction the ball will start.

2. Clubface alignment at impact controls which direction the

ball will curve in flight. (The exception is when playing from sand when the face contacts the sand, not the ball; in that case, the ball will follow the line of the swing).

3. Angle of attack (steep or shallow) influences the shot's trajectory (height) and, to some degree, its distance.

4. Speed of clubhead at impact determines distance the ball will fly for a given loft of club. It is worth noting that keeping the face square to the line of the swing produces the maximum possible distance, while opening or closing the face will reduce distance somewhat.

One more caveat. Some golf teachers insist upon including "swing plane" among the so-called laws of ball flight. Is it a fundamental? Not really; the fact is that plane has nothing to do with laws of ball flight, per se, and while we might argue its importance, it has no place here and will only cloud the picture. What we hope for here is clarity, not clouds; simplicity, not complexity.

These "laws" are the same for everyone, from Ernie Els and Annika Sorenstam to Lee Trevino and Mike Weir to you and me. Because they are immutable, we can profit by understanding them, yet it is probably better that we focus on the art of the thing than on the science. Fritz Kreisler, the great twentieth-century violinist, likened the experience of performance to a "sublime mystery." Sure, he had to practice to become a fine player, but the analysis of technique, said Kreisler, should remain a mystery, because at its most sublime, great performance IS a true mystery. Why is it any different for you and me? Have you not hit one or two glorious shots in your life? Isn't that a kind of mystery, or at times a miracle?

When the great men tell us, as Arnold Palmer does, that it is important to learn how to put your hands on the club so that it encourages rather than impedes a clean hit, or when they advise us, as Harvey Penick does, to get the feel of brushing the grass as we swing back and forth, or when they suggest, as Bob Jones does, that we are apt to hit longer and straighter shots if we can achieve an ease in our swing, they are telling us something useful. These things may not sound all that earth-shattering at first blush, but they are uttered by the gods and repeated by enough people who count that we probably can pay attention to their suggestions with some degree of confidence.

Within the context of the "ball flight laws," it is often the simplest things that help us most as we try to sort things out in our golf swings. To master the intricate physical motions is not always possible, given our individual differences and limitations, but it's a good deal simpler than we make it out to be. You may not be capable of hitting the ball as far as Phil Mickelson, but you don't need a golf swing that looks like his to drive a ball straight down the fairway. Anyone can hit the ball straight; not far, but straight. Wanna bet? Besides, the physical side of golf is a lot easier to work out than the mental side, as any good player will probably be willing to tell you. This conflict is built into the game, in case you hadn't noticed.

Chapter Four

Farewell the Tranquil Mind

"Whatever else golf may be, it is not a game; how much simpler life would be if it were." —-Peter Dobereiner

The appeal of golf is equally to our inner competitive natures and to the pull that nature exerts on us. There is a certain pathetic but never-ending fascination with pitting our puny selves against a natural world we view with admiration and envy, and a bit of fear. We are not moved alone by soaring tee shots; sometimes we are drawn to the long afternoon shadows, the newly mown grass, a beckoning flag, the shapes of the landscapes, and the changing elements. Golf's bards have touched on these things.

Arnold Haultain: "How beautiful the vacated links at dawn, when the dew gleams untrodden beneath the pendant flags and the long shadows lie quietly on the greens, and you stroll from hole to hole and drink in the beauties of a land to which you know you will be all too blind when the sun mounts high and you toss for the honor."

Bernard Darwin: "It is only in solitude and preferably in the dusk, when the lights begin to glimmer in the distant houses that practice is truly heavenly, and the nearest possible approach to the great secret of golf may be discovered."

These fellows lived in an age of purple prose, but how agreeably they expressed the many ways we internalize the game. The things they observed and wrote about are among the durable pleasures of golf, the images that bring us back because they satisfy something within us and soothe the pesky agitations of daily life.

Not one of his contemporaries doubted that Don January was a hard opponent whose competitive nature lacked any trace of sentiment or mercy. Nor would any of them have failed to recognize how the game had formed him. Growing up in Fort Worth, Texas, January didn't learn much about giving up or giving in. He might have had idols like Hogan and Nelson, local boys who made good, but those two were only measuring posts to set against one's own ambition. The game was always about beating something, somebody, anybody, mostly oneself.

January remembered: "When I was a kid, I'd put my bag on my shoulder and head for the golf course. I was there early, and they had to shoot a gun to get me off at night. It was dark and I was still trying to play. We'd play fifty-four holes or ninety or however many you could get in, just go round and round like it was a racetrack. It gets in your blood. It's you against that golf course, or mainly you against you. There's no harder competition than yourself. It's the greatest game I've ever played." The pleasures of the game.

Not much had changed by the time January's crowd turned fifty and the Senior Tour came along. As Don observed at the time:

"I've been trying to beat these same guys for thirty years, and it's still hard. But that's the fun of it. The competition; there's just no substitute for it. To be able to go out at our age and still play and feel the adrenaline in your veins, to give yourself the opportunity either to choke like hell or do something you're really not capable of doing. That's at the core of it, and it's the main reason we're playing. I'm like an old firehorse; you ring that bell and I'm ready."

Even hardened veterans like Don January fall under the curious spell of golf, a game that he admits got in his blood and stayed there.

The fires don't dim, but eventually the skills do. For about ten years on the big tour, January ranked among its top players. He won the PGA Championship and fourteen tournaments, and for another decade with the over-fifty crowd, always with his Texas pal Miller Barber, they became the leading lights on the fledgling Senior Tour. These two won more tournaments and more money on the senior tour than anyone, and when his time came, January went back to Fort Worth, put his legs up on a couch, his beloved cigarettes long gone, but a cool drink within easy reach.

"What do you do when you go home?" he was asked.

"Mostly, I rest," he replied. "I'm lazy, and I'm good at it, too." Hard to find fault with that.

Men like January waged their battles internally without much visible fuss or verbal dressing. They seemed more inclined to come to terms with life in their own way, in their own time. Nicklaus was like that. Others were not. In an interview with the *Palm Beach Post* in February of 2001, Greg Norman waxed optimistic about his return to the competitive golf wars after months of rehabilitation from shoulder surgery. Wouldn't it be something to see this attractive figure back at the top, we thought, even at the age of forty-six. After all, Greg pointed out, his great friend Jack Nicklaus had won the 1986 Masters at the same age. Why not me? he seemed to imply. Now that he was healthy, Norman admitted to reporters, his biggest battle was with his mind.

Ah, yes, the mind. The emotions and all that. Has anyone figured out, I wonder, why men like Greg Norman, Tom Weiskopf, Macdonald Smith, and Harry Cooper managed to fall just short of the grand achievements expected of them? Or men like Colin Montgomerie, Wild Bill Mehlhorn, and perhaps even Phil Mickelson? All of these fellows have had talent to burn, but usually lacked the stuff to finish it off. I'm not talking about the long list of Tony Maneros, Sam Parks, Jack Flecks, Herman Keisers, Vic Ghezzis, Orville Moodys, Wayne Gradys, Charles Coodys, Ed Furgols, Jeff Slumans, and Ian Baker-Finchs, each of whom had their moments in the sun. If Orville Moody had been blessed with the putting stroke of, say, Loren Roberts, his contemporaries will tell you that he'd have won ten majors, cold. And if Loren Roberts had owned the long game of Ernie Els, he might have won twenty. And if eagles could play harps, there'd be music in the sky. Well, there we are.

Few golfers had more raw ability and promise than Tom Weiskopf (left) or Greg Norman, each of whom won majors but each of whom also fell short of hopes and met disappointment from inner doubts or the whims of fate.

Weiskopf, Norman, and Cooper each won a bunch of tournaments and had nearly everything it takes to become dominant players except that last little bit of grit or heart or judgment that pushes the greatest ones ahead of the rest. Norman has had at least six majors in his grasp that fell away at the end, Weiskopf and Mickelson nearly as many. We who watch can almost taste the bitterness. In the wide open arena of professional golf, many with seemingly equal talent are not as fortunate even as these fellows have been in their successes. The game intrudes, the emotions rise, the brain begins its work, doubt appears, and confidence returns to its hiding place. Then, farewell the tranquil mind.

The most prominent recent example is David Duval. When Duval went into a deep slump following his victory in the 2001 British Open, neither Duval, nor his golf pro father, nor his colleagues on the PGA Tour could explain it or help him. The man who once shot 59 in competition, averaged 79 in the four majors in 2003, won no tournaments after July 2001, and fell from No. 1 to No. 250 in the world rankings. His fellow competitors shook their heads. Nick Price told the writer Jaime Diaz: "I'm beyond words when it comes to David. It's just very sad."

Acclaimed as one of the longest, straightest drivers on tour, Duval was now driving balls out-of-bounds, sometimes twice on a hole. He has always used a strong grip and, like Jim Furyk, has a highly individualized swing. Many have succeeded using idiosyncracies, including Duval himself. Speculation grew that he might retire from competition, although few with his talent can stay away for long. Duval is a thoughtful, reticent man, but his mind was obviously troubled by losing control of his game. He claimed the slump was caused by physical, not mental problems, and went seeking answers to famous swing guru, David Leadbetter, with the sympathy of every similarly afflicted golfer.

No one ever spent more time in the pursuit of swing knowledge and earned less for his trouble than

In winning the 2001 British Open, David Duval had touched the grail and seemed ready for stardom, then went into a puzzling slump from which he could find no easy escape.

George Schoux (pronounced Shoe). This tortured soul appeared on the tour briefly in the late 1940s and became something of a legend among his fellow pros. Schoux won a couple tour events, was a participant in the Goodall Round Robin (in those days, a prestigious event that invited only the top players), and in 1948 finished twenty-fourth on the money list. He had talent and a nice swing, but he was possessed by the idea of achieving perfect impact. Schoux hit balls incessantly, practiced in the dark, listened to all the top players, had vivid nightmares, and wore out his brain. He wound up in a mental institution, where he spent the rest of his days seeking the improbable. George Schoux made the pure striking of a golf ball his life's obsession. He's probably the only man we can cite today as having perished in the attempt.

Trying to analyze one's golf swing in too much detail can end in all kinds of misery. When the great Ralph Guldahl was asked to describe his swing, he became so confounded that his game, perhaps the most brilliant on the pro tour at the time, simply vanished, along with poor old Ralph. He was arguably the best Texan to gain prominence on the pro tour among a group that included Byron Nelson, Ben Hogan, Jimmy Demaret, Henry Ransom, and Lloyd Mangrum. In a span of four years, Guldahl won two U. S. Opens, one Masters, three Western Opens, then counted among the major championships, and did it apparently on pure instinct. When he tried to analyze his own swing so he could set it down on paper for a publisher, Ralph found he was not up to the task. The more he thought about it, the worse his game grew. Gene Sarazen thought Guldahl's downfall could be traced to "a tendency to close the face at contact, which his timing took care of for a number of years, but no longer could." Whatever the cause may have been, Guldahl crumbled mentally, left the tour, and finished his days as a club pro in California. Apparently, he could not face picking apart his own methods. Brad Faxon claimed something similar happened to his putting stroke during 2002 when he was asked to explain details of his much-admired technique in videotapes and books, so he stopped doing them. Paul Gaugin, the artist, once expressed his view of what happens in such cases:

Ralph Guldahl was the most dominant player in professional golf over a span of four glorious years, then watched it all melt away when he was asked to analyze his swing.

"Precision often destroys a dream, takes all the life out of a fable."

Yet we know, those of us bitten by the game, that obsession is absolutely central to golf. This seems to have been true from the very beginning, from the Parks and the Straths to the Palmers and Normans. We have seen the effects of this obsession on men like George Schoux, and on others like Bert Yancey and Phil McGlenno. Yancey appeared on tour with a brilliant game and silky putting stroke. He barely missed winning the U. S. Open in 1968 and fell just short in three Masters between 1967 and 1970. He was so obsessed with the Masters that he built miniature replicas of the Augusta National holes in his basement so he could plot his strategy. He was found one day muttering and wandering aimlessly in an airline terminal and was mercifully hauled away to a nearby psychiatric ward. Eventually he was diagnosed and treated for manic-depression. So intent was McGlenno on plumbing the secrets of the game that he went to live in the California desert, changed his name to Mac O'Grady, began communing with the planets, and eventually established himself as a kind of oracular swing guru.

Alistair Cooke, the eminently sensible writer and host of Masterpiece Theater for all those years, was another fellow hopelessly taken with the game. Nearing retirement after twenty-two years as a television host, what were his plans? "I have an insane desire to shave a stroke or two off my golf handicap," said Cooke, with a crooked gleam.

Bert Yancey (at left, seated with Billy Casper during the 1970 Masters) was a brilliant prospect but was driven toward perfection and winning at Augusta, and soon fell victim to his mental demons.

OBSESSION AND TEMPER

The line between these obsessions is not easily drawn and even less easily understood. The one between George Schoux and Ben Hogan, in fact, is particularly fine. Hogan was so driven to succeed that he spent his entire days—and much of his nights— thinking about and experimenting with his swing. His friends were few and almost always kept at a distance. His wife, Valerie, took care of the usual details while Hogan practiced and competed. When Hogan built his house in Fort Worth, a fine, spacious one, it had only one bedroom because, the story goes, Ben preferred not to take chances that a visitor or relative might want to stay the night. Yet Hogan was a genial fellow in conversation (though he did not suffer fools), was genuinely liked by his peers, went out of his way to be candid (but careful) with the press, and knew how to both lose and win with grace, although he hated to lose. Somehow Hogan's obsession made room for social niceties like dancing (like many fine golfers, he was a superb dancer), gambling, complimenting women on their attire, and delivering delightful, eloquent speeches at professional gatherings. But nothing interfered with his obsession.

George Schoux, by contrast, seems to have been more possessed than obsessed. Although raised in California, Schoux made his way east, as so many aspiring pros did in those days, to serve as an assistant under Claude Harmon at Winged Foot Golf Club, in Mamaroneck, New York. Schoux was slender, stood about five-feet-nine, and had a slashing swing vaguely like that of his idol, Ben Hogan. He had peculiar habits, among them that of holding a cigarette between the first two fingers of his right hand while putting. According to Jack Burke Jr., who served as an assistant pro at Winged Foot about the same time, George had a little fellow, a sort of doll, that he'd carry around in his pocket with the fingers visible clasping the top of the fabric while its eyes peeked over the edge. He'd talk to the little fellow between shots, and on other occasions.

"Shoux would practice all the time, even at night when he'd stack flashlights all around the putting green," Burke recalled. "He would arch his wrist way over to take out any movement in the putting stroke."

George Schoux (right) is congratulated by PGA tour manager Fred Corcoran after winning his first tournament. He won again but grew obsessed with the golf swing, practiced in the dark, and eventually broke under the strain.

Schoux tried the tour in 1947 and won his first tournament, the Richmond Open, at the Richmond, California Country Club, whose field included big guns Jimmy Demaret, Lloyd Mangrum, Ben Hogan, Chick Harbert, Jim Turnesa and Lew Worsham. He was on his way. That year Schoux finished second to Jim Turnesa in the North and South Open in Pinehurst, then considered, with the Western Open, one of the major events of the year. He went on to finish runner-up at Charlotte, third in the Inverness Four-Ball with Ed Furgol as partner, and thirty-eighth in the Masters. In 1948, he placed third at St. Petersburg, fifth at Albuquerque, qualified for the U. S. Open, placing forty-first, and finished twenty-fourth on the money list.

George Schoux had moved into the charmed circle. He had the game, the putting stroke, and the Hogan-like swing action. In January 1949 George Schoux won again, but then something happened. He finished thirty-sixth at Tucson, lost in the first round of the Miami Four-Ball with Jackie Burke as a partner and began talking to himself and the little friend he carried around in his pocket. He was seen hitting balls on the practice tee most of the day and into the nights. Arnold Palmer, still an amateur, was making his first appearance in a professional event at the Dapper Dan Tournament near Pittsburgh that year. Arnold was nineteen and finished last in a field of fifty-four, but he remembered Schoux.

"George Schoux drove his car onto the eighteenth hole, aimed his headlights down the fairway, and practiced in the middle of the night," Arnold said. Not long afterward, Schoux vanished. His absence was noticed by a few of the players, but no one seemed to know where he had gone. It turned out that Schoux had returned to San Francisco and Sharp Park, a public course where his brother, Al, was the pro.

There is more to the story of George Schoux. Some say he served in the Navy during World War II where he was a shipboard welder, and barely survived an explosion below decks, which may have affected him. Others say he tried to recapture his game at Sharp Park, but one day while reaching into the cup to retrieve his ball he yanked out his hand, claiming that the hole was filled with writhing snakes. Whatever the truth, his remaining days were spent in a mental hospital in Santa Clara, California, with occasional afternoons hitting golf balls at Sharp Park with his brother

Al's buddies, and perhaps dreaming of his brief moments of glory and his unhappy pursuit of the perfect swing.

To be fair, very few golfers, including the best, have tranquil minds as part of their original factory equipment. Those overcome by doubts rarely survive. Most come fully equipped with tempers and a healthy dose of impatience, especially as youngsters, and they aren't shy about showing them. In a word, they're hotheads. After you've murdered a shot, what could feel better than whacking the next one 300 yards? Or after handing an opponent a sickly gift in the middle of a match, isn't there something reassuring about a scorching temper that starts things going again? Golfers nowadays might imagine that Jack Nicklaus and Bobby Jones were perfectly behaved tykes, but Jones, Sarazen, Palmer, and Nicklaus all were hotheads once.

Jones and Sarazen met as teenagers when both were club throwers and made a famous bet that the first man to throw a club would collect ten dollars from the other. After a spell, Sarazen thought he had a winner. Jones hit a miserable shot, and Gene turned to his caddie: "Watch, there goes his club and here comes my ten bucks." But Jones held it in, and didn't have to pay. "I never saw him throw a club again," said Sarazen, although Jones later admitted to a few relapses, but never in public.

"Once in a while, I'd let one fly, and I got a great deal of relief from it, too, if you want the truth," Jones confessed. Tommy Bolt and Steve Pate would surely understand.

Arnold Palmer and Jack Nicklaus had as much spirit as other teenagers, perhaps more, but their fathers made it clear that cursing or tossing clubs on the golf course would mean banishment from golf. They meant it, too, so the sons learned very early how

Gene Sarazen (left) and Bob Jones formed a lifelong friendship after meeting as teenagers when both were temperamental club-throwers. They made a famous wager over who would be the first to heave one in public, a bet that Jones almost lost.

to channel their anger. It wasn't only a question of good manners; the fathers knew that athletes—boxers, say—who are ruled by emotions or visions of grandeur usually wind up on their backsides, a lesson that cannot be learned too early. On the other hand, they probably knew that a healthy temper is a motivator and a useful thing to have, you might even say an essential one. The trick is to learn how to turn it to your own purposes.

The same could be said for learning how and when to bend confidence to your wishes. Too much of that stuff is not always a good thing. Confidence and ability often go together, and no one had more of these than Phil Mickelson did when he turned professional. His skills seemed a match for almost anyone in golf—a marvelous touch in the short game, enormous distance with wood, and superlative abilities with iron. He won more than his share as a professional, yet his inability to capture major events mystified his fans. Other players had gone years before winning the big events, but today's fans are less patient. Most troubling, the left-hander found ways to crumple on the final holes of majors by making what appeared to be mental rather than physical errors.

Perhaps it is something else entirely. Much has been made of Mickelson's aggressive instincts and his willingness to encourage them. Rather too much, in Phil's eyes. Things boiled to a head during the 2002 Players Championship in Ponte Vedra Beach, Florida, when the press questioned his unwillingness to play more carefully on such a difficult golf course. Mickelson had had enough, and told the press: "I've been criticized for my style of play, but it's won me twenty tournaments and given me lots of opportunities in the majors, so I won't ever change. Not tomorrow. Not Sunday. Not at Augusta or the U. S. Open or any other event."

Which means that he would, one felt. The time would come when the pulled driver into the woods, the six-iron over the green, the too-bold putt that runs eight feet past and then is missed on the return, when all of this would cost him too dearly. Possibly it would come when he saw time running out and realized he was not destined to win a major event without changing his creative but destructive style of attack.

The transformation came in the 2004 Masters, a tournament in which Mickelson curbed his wilder impulses, played for good position on fairway and green, and won by holing a brave putt of eighteen feet at the end to edge Ernie Els by a stroke. Whether or not Phil's conversion is permanent, this we know about golf at the top: To become an acknowledged master rather than a carnival performer is to temper the raw instincts of talent and emotion and channel them into a kind of cold-blooded, efficient performance

After a decade of trying to win a major, a stubborn but enormously-talented Phil Mickelson tamed his aggressive impulses to capture the 2004 Masters, a masterful performance marked by discipline and control.

that is marked as much by control as by inspiration. As great concert pianists and violinists do, the greatest golfers learn that emotion, ego, and personality will carry performance only so far, and that discipline is not the enemy but their greatest friend. They also learn that impatience is a killer of talent.

In his autobiography, Bob Jones admitted to playing every shot for all he could, regardless of risk, until William Fownes, the cagey veteran from Oakmont who had won the 1910 Amateur Championship, offered him a gentle word of advice. "Bob, you've got to learn that the best shot possible is not always the best shot to play." Jones said that this was a hard lesson to learn, but he acknowledged he didn't start winning the big events until learning "to adjust my ambitions to more reasonable prospects rather than placing my hopes upon accomplishing a series of brilliant sallies." When the old wilderness tramp Henry David Thoreau was asked what he had learned from living in the woods, he replied, "It is characteristic of wisdom not to do desperate things."

TAMING THE NERVES

A century ago Harry Vardon had an idea about what happens with men like Mickelson and Jones.

"Golf, for all the appearance of tame tranquility it may present to the uninitiated mind, provides a more searching test of nerve and temperament than any other game in the world." This led, said Vardon, to two distinct classes of player, the one who could win championships and the other who could not, and there is no way to account for the difference. He went on: "Of all games, golf is the one that comes nearest to being an art. It is pursued with deliberation and method; its inspirations are the player's own creation, since he is never called upon to strike a moving ball. It demands the greatest delicacy and accuracy of touch, as well as power to hit hard. An art requires a sensitive nervous system, and in golf the difference between the two classes of players to which I have referred is that the one can keep his nerves under control during the most trying period, and the other cannot." Maybe the game hasn't changed as much as we think.

One of the maddening things about golf is its unreasonable insistence that we tame the demons inside before it allows us to get very far. Golfers devise any number of ways to cast doubts, however tiny or fleeting, from their minds. Trevino talks, Mickelson stalks, Chi Chi dances a jig, Nicklaus glares, Wadkins hurries, Faldo doesn't, Demaret beamed at the crowds, Hogan withdrew from them. Rich Beem demonstrated that he had no fear of parties, nor of golf immortals either, when he snatched the 2002 PGA Championship out of Tiger Woods's hands while swigging Pepto Bismol to soothe his nerves. Brave but nervous. Julius Boros moved slowly, sort of like a Moose, which was his nickname on the pro tour. He had a reputation as an easygoing fellow, the Big Easy of his day, and was always at his best in the big money events. But inside, he seethed. He dragged the club inside with a languid move that proved very efficient for his well-upholstered frame because it allowed him to conserve energy and at the same time hit the hell out of the ball. This inspired one of author Charley Price's better lines: "The lazy grace with which he makes the golf course come to him, rather than he to it, enraptures me."

Bernard Darwin offered an insight into the highly-strung golfer. In describing Vardon's great rival J. H. Taylor, Darwin wrote: "J. H. never could or would take the game lightheartedly and

Harry Vardon (left) and James Braid, two thirds of the great triumvirate, are shown in 1912, both having won five Open Championships. Vardon would win once more, in 1914. Braid was described as a big-hearted man who could take a defeat with an even disposition.

never for a moment pretended that he did. He fought the enemy, he fought himself, he fought the very fates, and from this triple fray emerged triumphant. His career bears witness to the fact that the highly strung man who can master himself will rise to heights never to be reached by those with more lethargic pulses."

Andrew "Andra" Kirkaldy was a fixture at St. Andrews for fifty years and a great match player, though never able to win The Open. He was a man of ready mirth, a renowned storyteller and a hardy old warrior who called a spade a spade. He dismissed those who would offer excuses: "The petted little men who mope and mourn when things go against them will never do much good at anything." He contrasted these with the men of big hearts and settled spirits, like his contemporary James Braid, who he described as a man "who can take a defeat and take a good meal after it." One can't help but want to see more of Braid in the modern sports figures.

Stoics or not, golf will always have its nervous souls. There have been the fidgets like Cary Middlecoff, a Hall of Famer for all of his fussy mannerism, and today's version, Sergio Garcia. The popular Spaniard went through a notorious patch of milking the grip before every shot, up to thirty times on drives, fourteen to sixteen times on shorter irons. After rising complaints from fellow pros and the press, Garcia decided to eliminate the mannerism in time for the 2002 Masters, although he resumed the habit briefly during the U. S. Open later that season. Sergio said he fell into the habit of regripping to help establish a "feel" for the shot he was about to play. His opponents got to where they wouldn't watch. Scott McCarron said after one tournament: "I watched the tops of trees, clouds, stared at blades of grass, drank some water, read the paper, all kinds of stuff." Blades of grass; there's something to put you in the right mood. Asked if he had timed Sergio's waggles, Jack Nicklaus deadpanned: "No, my watch stopped in the middle." This remark from the old tour's slowest member might strike some of Jack's contemporaries as hilarious.

Sergio's mannerism is not new. Sandy Herd, who was a constant thorn in the side of Vardon, Taylor, and Braid, is said to have waggled fourteen times before each shot. Why fourteen and not thirteen or fifteen is not explained, but the habit obviously helped Herd to one Open Championship and three second-place finishes in a career that lasted from 1895 to 1920. More recently, Cary Middlecoff milked the handle until his opponents either fell asleep or passed out and Hubert Green jerked the club up and down like a pump handle before pulling the trigger. Among today's players, Jesper Parnevik and Jose Maria Olazabal each have displayed mild cases on occasion, but nothing like the tortured deliberations of players such as the terminally careful David Frost, Padraig Harrington, who has been called "the human rain delay," or Glen "All" Day, a nickname bestowed by tour caddies for the time he takes to play a shot. Nicklaus was a dawdler who later admitted his transgressions. During his prime, Jack would hit no golf shot before its time. His fellow pros spoke to him about his slow playing habits without much effect, although one rumor, if true, might have turned the trick—a caddie wanted to paint a big, red stop sign on the bottom of his MacGregor golf bag as a prank.

The truth is that nobody is a fast player anymore because the PGA Tour doesn't allow it. Lanny Wadkins, one of the game's fastest players, and others of his ilk reached the point where they couldn't bear the laggard pace of a tour event anymore. Why not? Because tour officials refused to enforce the rules for fear of disqualifying a popular player. The tour has had a policy against slow play for decades, providing a stroke penalty for violations, but it's not even honored in the breach; in all that time, not one player has been slapped with the hated stroke, even when he deserved it. To disqualify someone for a scorecard error is okay because the evidence is right there in black and white and no one can blame the rules official; but to yank Nicklaus or another star off the fairway in 1970? Are you kidding? When P. J. Boatwright, the late, intrepid USGA executive director, levied two strokes on John Schroeder at the 1981 U. S. Open at Merion, the executive committee arbitrarily overruled him, reinforcing the regrettable trend.

Perhaps as they dawdle, Bernhard Langer, Sergio Garcia, Bob Estes, and the rest of the fidgets are merely seeking their own patch of tranquility, their moment of inspiration. Who can forget the grim tableaux of Ben Hogan at the end of his career, standing over his putts for what seemed an eternity because, as he candidly admitted, he was trying to screw up the courage to draw back the blade? At the end, this consummate ball striker dreaded the greens, those targets that for him were so accessible, because they had become hollow stages where all tranquil thoughts would vanish.

COACHES AND GURUS

Among the more cerebral paths being trod by modern competitive golfers is the one that leads directly to coaches. You aren't considered a proper player anymore without a swing teacher or a guru of some sort. Promising amateurs nowadays seem to sign them on before puberty. This seems to have as much to do with keeping a sound mind as having a sound swing. Lee Trevino once hooted: "I'll hire a swing coach when I find one who can beat me." Gary Player says he does not understand why a good player would need one. Gary was quoted in *Golf World* as saying that "having someone standing there giving me lessons would drive me nuts." He implied that Nick Faldo's problems after winning six majors may

Lee Trevino had little good to say about swing coaches. His own, unorthodox swing produced shotmaking of superb quality; students of golf swings claim that his club stayed on line longer than anyone since Hogan.

have originated with coaching. "Some of these coaches can't break 75, yet they can coach a world champion. I can't comprehend that," Gary snapped. He's right, of course, but isn't this the same fellow who for forty years had a reputation for owning the biggest ears among the top pros? Gary Player would cock an ear to grocery clerks, motorcycle cops, and barroom sweeps if any of them whispered a fast tip on just about any aspect of the golf swing. He didn't need to, you understand, but wanted to know, just in case.

The game's mental gurus have flourished in recent years and are becoming more of a fixture than a fad on the pro tour. From Tim Gallwey, Richard Coop, and Bob Rotella, the game's younger crowd is turning to its own generation of gurus, like Gio Valiante, a brilliant young professor of psychology at Rollins College in Winter Park, Florida, who has come up with new data that fascinates and attracts many of the pros. A less academic approach is used by the Belgian Jos Vandisphout, a former rock musician who coaches South African stars Ernie Els and Retief Goosen. The mental gurus have become as thick on the ground as agents. Fellows like Snead and Hogan wouldn't have bothered, although when I asked Sam once if he'd consider using a psychologist, he pursed his lips and said: "Uh, can he putt?" Jackie Burke had a simple take on this subject: "Jimmy Demaret and I had the best golf psychologist in the world. His name was Jack Daniels, and he was waiting for us after every round."

It's pretty clear that the modern players want reasons for just about everything. Players like Snead, Trevino, Ballesteros, and Mangrum never paid much attention to reasons; they looked for results. They didn't look at golf swings, not even Snead's; they paid attention to what the ball did and where it went. The key word for them was "Play"—play to learn, and learn to play. This was how Dutch Harrison and Peter Thomson and Julius Boros and Bruce Lietzke learned. That's still the best way for young golfers to learn, although there is so much more knowledge available these days in every form—books, television, videos—and more first-class teachers. During a recent televised golf tournament, the announcer said of Irishman Padraig Harrington: "It's not a swing that would win any beauty contests, but it works." Well, that's the idea, isn't it?

PRACTICE MAKES WHAT?

And then there is practice. Some players think it's essential, others believe it does little good. Among the great practicers have been Ben Hogan, Vijay Singh, Dave Hill, Brad Bryant, the notorious Dr. Dirt, and the unfortunate George Schoux. Those opposed include Cary Middlecoff, Bob Rosburg, Carlos Franco, Chris DiMarco, and the most famous non-practicer of all, Bruce Lietzke. Bob Rosburg won the PGA Championship in 1959 without ever visiting the practice range. Sam Snead never went quite that far, but preferred to practice by playing. Whether playing in an exhibition or a tournament, or dodging between foursomes to find an open hole while plucking a few pigeons back at The Greenbrier, Sam probably played an average of thirty-six holes every day of his life until he was well into his eighties.

In 1991 John Daly jumped from obscurity to trample the field and win the PGA Championship at Crooked Stick, in Indiana, establishing another of golf's improbable and delightful legends. Can anyone remember who finished second? Bruce Lietzke was the man, and had Daly not appeared from nowhere, the practice ranges of America might not have recovered from a Lietzke victory. The long and short of it is, Lietzke is one of those freaks of nature who can put aside his clubs for weeks or months and suffer no ill effects when he resumes playing. His rather unorthodox swing is a symphony of grooved precision and constancy; every shot he hits is a controlled fade, and he does it at least as well as Hogan did, maybe better, because Hogan had to practice.

Lietzke's steady left-to-right ball flight pattern led to his nickname of Leaky. The famous story of his caddie finding a rancid banana in his golf bag after two month's vacation, placed there during the pair's last tournament outing, is true. Lietzke hadn't touched the bag during the long layoff. For many years, Bruce spent the early part of the year on tour, competing until he collected enough prize money, then returned to Texas to pursue other interests. The Leaky One views professional golf as a means to make a living, and prefers to spend time with his family or fishing or collecting automobiles, and who can blame him? A case could be made that he is one of greatest natural golfers in history, although his putting is not quite in the same class as his ball striking.

Few swing zealots will be satisfied with Bruce Lietzke's disdain for practice, however, nor are they likely to be blessed with his talent. More of us are apt to follow the unhappy George Schoux to perdition. In that event, we might recall something Bernard Darwin observed about practice: "The body always does its best; it learns as quickly as it can, and it does not like orders being rubbed in too hard. You can, so to speak, tell it gradually less and trust gradually more to its memory."

Those willing to learn the game can expect setbacks now and again. Anxious types who are impatient with lessons and learning are probably the same sort who would expect to speak fluent Turkish after one lesson. When Luciano Pavarotti was twelve, he met the legendary Italian tenor Beniamino Gigli, who many believe had been the greatest lyric tenor of all. Gigli was then fifty-seven and was about to give another sold-out concert. Pavarotti asked how long the great man had studied to become such an accomplished singer. Replied Gigli: "I have only stopped about five minutes ago." A Hogan man, obviously.

Bruce Lietzke wallows in his collection of automobiles at his home in Plano, Texas. The Leaky One prefers this to practice and only appears at tournaments to collect his due, a nice check for another high finish.

As for the rest of the crowd, beginners and students and good golfers alike, do we expect too much of ourselves? Do we load the mind with more than it can bear? Consider the parallels in golf and music. Jazz historian Nat Hentoff found himself in conversation with a pianist about the many different ways jazz musicians can find to play a song. He was fascinated by something the great horn player Dizzy Gillespie had told him: "There are infinite ways of playing a song, and I keep trying ways I hadn't thought of before. There's always something new to explore in music." The pianist friend, Hank Jones, nodded: "That's exactly right, and that's why every day I begin again."

I suppose that's a pretty fair description of what happens with golfers, although some of us would be satisfied to find just one way, and that it would be as faithful to us as we are to it.

CHAPTER
FIVE

GOLFERS ARE BORN LOSERS

"Our business in life is not to succeed, but to continue to fail in good spirits." —Robert Louis Stevenson

The Germans, who have a way with such persistent human impulses as music and sacred beliefs, have a proverb that goes: "God gave us music that we might pray without words." In a contrary vein, we can say the Scots gave us golf that we might suffer without guilt. This arises from the concept of golf as honest suffering; that is, to experience inward pain and humiliation unencumbered by either excuse or blame. It can also be seen as a plain acceptance of our fallibility and mortality and of that tiny place assigned to us by a rude Nature.

The noted Gaelic scholar David Feherty claims golfers are born losers. This is true even on the pro tour. He points out that figures as heroic as Snead and Nicklaus actually lost ninety percent of the time. This is a hard rock to swallow when your talent and ego are enormous, which covers most of the great ones. The game drives the pros berserk, because a man can post a score of 65 playing better than humanity should allow and still lose by two strokes to some brainless clod who has holed fourteen consecutive putts. This happens all the time on the pro tour, which is why you hear the pros mutter that tour events are largely putting contests.

David Feherty, a television commentator now, points out that Hogan and Nicklaus lost ninety percent of the time, which makes them and us born losers.

The pros are driven berserk because they know they can hit every shot, and still they lose far more than they win. The amateur, for the most part, is driven berserk because he *cannot* hit every shot, although his ego tells him he bloody well should, and he cannot imagine why the secret eludes him. The difference between the two, pro and amateur, is between the one who knows he can beat anyone on earth and the other who dreams that he might. For example, when Arnold Palmer joined the pro tour in the mid-1950s, he always expressed the greatest respect for a man like Ben Hogan, still a mighty figure in golf. But Palmer never doubted, not for a moment, that he could beat him.

Whether or not this was the whole truth is beside the point, because most of the time, no matter what they say publicly, these men feel in their bones that they cannot be beaten by anyone. So when they meet their match, as they always do, they can find no acceptable excuse other than that a quirk of fate or a gust of wind has intervened, that the opponent has holed two improbable shots from the fairway that he oughtn't, or that he has been distracted at a critical moment; in short, that the game is unpredictably and madly berserk. And, of course, it is. The professional tends to blame outside agencies like fate, a traitorous putter, or a blade of grass. The amateur, lacking a degree of confidence, tends to internalize the blame, shouldering responsibility for a lunge in the downswing, a slice into the woods, or a stabbed chip. Though an honest fellow, his repeated failures understandably drive him mad.

THE 'RULES,' IS IT?

Amateurs and professionals are alike in one respect, however; both must deal with the Rules of Golf, such as they are. These commandments, once held in a place of honor but now often scorned, are presently enshrined with their "decisions" in a massive volume the size of Rhode Island which contains enough interpretations, exceptions, explanations, and amendments to keep a battalion of lawyers off the streets for life. We seem to need them, though, in a culture that looks with ever more disdain upon anyone who is not a clear winner. Today we watch professionals compete in tournaments that allow them to touch the ball on almost any pretext, and my own eyes have seen spectators enlisted to move a massive boulder from a player's path with the connivance of the PGA Tour field staff. My, my what would Tom Morris or

Bobby Jones or Richard Tufts, that grand guardian of the Rules, make of that sort of thing?

Charles Price was one of our best writers on golf and a good enough player in his own right to take his game to the pro tour for a brief interlude during the late 1940s, before he came to his senses and founded a golf magazine. In Charley's cranky piece on the Rules of Golf, he boiled the commandments down to their simplest form. "For all intents and purposes, the early rules can be reduced to three," Charley wrote. "1. Don't touch your ball after you have teed it up until it goes in the hole. 2. If your ball lands in the rough, don't bend over. 3. If your ball flies into the woods, keep clapping your hands until you find it. In other words, don't cheat." This sentiment echoes Walter Simpson's ancient reminder that "after leaving the tee, you are not allowed to do anything to the ball except strike it or swear at it until you have either given up the hole or got to the bottom of it." If you want to play golf, laddies and lassies, there'll be no touching, if you please.

Modern corruptions of the rules, legal but sneaky, only under-score what golfers face in their frail efforts to master a game that cannot be mastered. Once the game has grabbed hold of some-one, you'd be amazed at the rationalizations that come popping out of the woods, so to speak, or at a golfer's willingness to make grand excuses for the smallest bending of a rule, or to find just cause for removing any one of nature's thousand inconvenient obstacles, large or small. It's not that we are lawless, mind you, but rather are desperate for salvation. Though we chase the ghosts of perfect swings and golfing heroes, we know we're eternal los-ers, and the devil take anyone or any legislation that stands in our way.

THE 'NECESSITIES'

One reads of the qualities needed to be a great golfer, such as concentration, composure, attitude, determination, and the rest. What nonsense. Only three things are of much use to an athlete—arrogance, a certain kind of intelligence, and talent. All the rest is twaddle, and of these, talent is the most needed. From arrogance flows determination, confidence, an appetite for domination, and composure. From intelligence flows attitude, a will to win, patience, and concentration. From talent one may be lucky enough to obtain speed, hand-eye coordination, and strength, and from the last, stamina.

"You can't advise talent," declared Oscar Levant, who had plenty and understood that talent usually finds its own way. Tommy Armour listed the capacity to take bad breaks without getting upset third behind talent and intelligence ("the kind of intelligence that fits the sport," he said) as qualities needed for golf, and I won't argue with that. Anything else? Well, judgment, yes, which might seem to flow from intelligence but too many otherwise intelligent people lack that quality for this to be true. Judgment, or rather the capacity for it, is acquired over time, isn't it? and by much trial and error. Byron Nelson put this business another way in an introduction he wrote in 1987 for a facsimile edition of John Low's classic, *Concerning Golf*: "To be good at golf, you have to have patience, determination and good concentration, but if you don't have these qualities when you start, golf will teach them to you." I suppose Byron meant this to be encouraging, but he might just as well have added that golf also teaches us without pity to know our limitations, and to face them honorably.

So, if you lack any of the three or four essential qualities, it's a good bet that you're a born loser like the rest of us. It will be seen fairly quickly, though, that arrogance and intelligence fail to equal talent. No degree of bluster, and no amount of prissy swing principles nor of learning the fine points of the game will cover for the lack of talent. We know this with shattering certainty when we watch Snead or Trevino or Woods play a round of golf. Their long shots are almost always im-

Never mind the awesome power and distance achieved by golfers like Tiger Woods (above), it's the way they play the little shots that convinces us of the truth—they come from another planet.

pressive, it's true, but it's the way they play the little shots that convinces us of the awful truth—we'll never be able to play like those guys. Adam Scott, the Australian phenom, hits the ball about as far as Tiger does, but three splendid little chips in the last four holes are the strokes that gave him the 2004 Players Championship. By the way, if you think Snead couldn't match the others around the green, just ask the men he played against. When the talent was passed around, everyone in this group came away with a full cupboard. We have seen, too, that talent served without the sauce of judgment is a very cold dish.

PLAYERS VS. GOLFERS

The pros know the difference between those who are merely accomplished and those who are feared. In the first category are those who have earned a certain respect for their skills, as in, "He's a real good player." In the second category, the phrase you are apt to hear is, "He can play." Implicit in this assertion is an acknowledgment that the fellow is routinely capable of low scoring and is most dangerous when it matters. When the accent falls on the last word, we are describing true genius, as in, "Harvie Ward could PLAY." In extreme cases when admiration overcomes vocabulary, the word "really" will be used, as in, "Demaret could really play," with emphasis on the penultimate word. You don't

Arnold Palmer eyes Harvie Ward (right) before their semifinal match in the 1948 North and South Amateur. Both guys could *really* play, although this time Ward played better, beating Arnold, and then Frank Stranahan in the finals.

often hear the pros use the word 'great' to describe other players, except in the general sense when referring to who the great players were. Why bother to mention that Casper or Snead was a great player? No need to state the obvious.

THAT LOOK

There is also "that look," a combination of withering stare and cold dismissal that so many of the great ones seem to have. Hogan and Snead had it. Middlecoff had it, and so did Mangrum and Casper, and Nicklaus always. Raymond Floyd had it, and so did Wadkins. Sarazen and Runyan had it, and sometimes Watson, too, but not always. Tom Kite, for all his wonderful ability, has not the look; in fact, no one born after 1950 ever had it except for Woods, who almost has it. A sparkle never seems far from Tiger's expression, and his natural inclination is to find humor in things. This flaw is usually packed away when he is on the prowl for birdies and tournament scalps, but there it is. Curtis Strange seemed like he wanted to have it, although one had the impression that it was imposed sometimes on an unwilling nature. It's a look that announces the guy as someone who would eat your children, take their lunch money, and toss their bones over a cliff.

No one born after 1950 has "the look," a cold stare that seemed to be standard equipment with veteran pros like (left to right) Ben Hogan and Lloyd Mangrum, and sometimes amateurs like Sean Connery.

Golf, especially the brand played at the competitive level, contains within it room to express all the human foibles and some of the traits we'd rather hide. It shouldn't surprise us when we see streaks of cruelty, gluttony, anger, and pride creep into our behavior because the game so often tempts us to give in to them. One of the reasons we're fond of golf is the opportunity it affords us to give in to our emotions, as we feel perfectly entitled to do, and then rise above them, as we know we must if we hope to prevail.

IT'S A GAME, ISN'T IT?

Golf appeals to many of us—man, woman, child, beginner, or expert—on so many different levels we sometimes forget it's a game. The game is not always a matter of thrusting a long eagle putt into the hole, even when it plunges the dagger into an opponent's heart. Sometimes it is the more subtle business of taking the course with a single weapon, a seven-iron perhaps, and discovering how many ways there are to play a hole.

We take ourselves altogether too seriously as a rule, but in golf it gets pretty thick sometimes. Especially nowadays, the drama tends to be trowelled into the newspapers and golf magazines with a heavy hand and even makes its way into golf telecasts. Here is a dialog that occurred during a broadcast of the third round of the 2001 PGA Championship:

Ernie Johnson, TNT anchor: "Now back to the second tee. Let's see if someone in this threesome can hit a fairway." He's referring to the pairing of Tiger Woods, David Duval, and Retief Goosen, each of whom has missed the opening fairway with their tee shots.

Bill Kratzert, a TNT commentator, watching Woods and Duval miss again:

"Well, we're oh-for-five…and now we're oh-for-six because this one is huge right; it's gonna fly into the trees," describing a wild

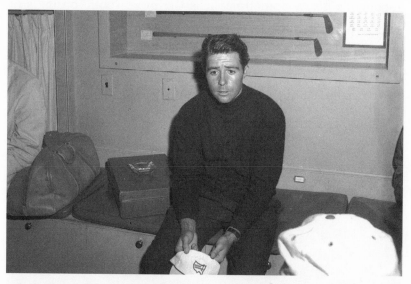

"Golf is sorrow," said Gary Player after winning the PGA Championship with a wizard shot. All the poor man could think about was the misery of golf, while other great players have called it a game of regrets.

slice by Goosen. So far, so good, but then Bobby Clampett, another TNT commentator, proclaims darkly: "That is a miserable feeling." He pauses: "A lonely feeling." Another pause: "A helpless one."

Ernie Johnson's voice intones: "You are not alone."

A moment of dead air is followed by the lilting voice of David Feherty: "Guys, it's only a game. Let's not get suicidal here."

Golfers do tend to be melodramatic, even morbid when their hopes are frustrated. Gary Player once moaned, "Golf is sorrow!" or rather a series of sorrows, and this was after winning the PGA Championship in Detroit one year. Just imagine, the guy wins with a Harry Potter wizard shot over a willow tree in the drizzling rain on the most dangerous hole on the toughest course in America, and all he remembers is the misery he faced. Jay Hebert, a lovely man with a lovely swing, was himself a PGA Champion who had a similar, though less dramatic take on this. "You might say that golf is a game of regrets. If you had used that other swing instead of this one; if only you had played it boldly, or if only you hadn't. That old 'if' never seems to leave you in this game. Not a day goes by that you don't regret something in this game. But that 'if' business won't get it, because golf is mostly a game of decisions. Everybody on the pro tour has the shots, so it's a matter of making the right decision at the right time." Can the answer be to think positively, to be decisive, and to imagine ourselves capable of something more? Well, maybe a little more of that sort of thing wouldn't hurt.

THE IDEAL PLAYER

If I imagined myself the ideal golfer and I could ask for everything, I would ask for these: the hands of Hogan, the heart of Nelson, the body of Snead, the mind of Thomson, the disposition of Mangrum, the pluck and the luck of Sarazen, the putting of Locke, and the swing, naturally, of Snead. Bolt's might be the swing you would pick, but it did not have the power of Hogan nor would it last as long as Snead's. Armed with these, I would not need the talent of Woods or the confidence of Nicklaus. A few implements and any golf course will do. Would you care to play for something? For the national debt, perhaps? For the Louvre? Or Switzerland?

I wouldn't need the boldness of Palmer, nor the resourcefulness of Ford. When would I get in trouble? What could I fear? Snead would get me on any hole in two, Nelson would drive me onward, Locke would hole everything, and the brainy Thomson would see to it that everything was sorted out properly. And every now and again, Sarazen might hole me a four-wood or something. Let's see, three times eighteen makes 54. There would be no reason to score higher than that, even on bad days. One might even get a few holes-in-one, although adding Art Wall to the list would hardly be fair. Even so, rounds in the forties would be routine. Never mind Switzerland; how about Dallas?

Don't laugh; it is our dreams that urge us on. They tantalize and taunt us. Ben Hogan once had a dream that beats most of yours. According to Jimmy Demaret, who would know because he was sleeping in the next bunk, Hogan kept grinding his teeth all night so loudly and fiercely that Demaret feared for his friend's well-being. Besides, the grating noise kept waking him up. He shook Ben, who awoke with an angry groan. "What's the matter?" asked Demaret. "I was having a dream, the perfect round," Hogan rasped. "I didn't miss a shot; knocked the first drive straight into the cup, and made a one at each of the next sixteen holes. I came to the last, a tight par-four, hit a long drive way down the fairway that bounded along and rolled onto the green following the contours of the ground. I read it perfectly, too, and just before you woke me, the sonuvabitch lipped out."

This is the dream of a young man, full of himself, who believes he must and will prevail. But the greatest players, as Professor Feherty observed, lose far more often than they win—Nicklaus, Vardon, Snead, Nelson, and Woods today. Each week they chase the grail, and even in the act of seizing it, they know they are losers. In a moment of diffident candor, David Duval confided to the writer Tom Callahan that a sense of inadequacy followed him all the time. "Golf is a game of getting used to failure, isn't it? And at the same time, fighting against it, becoming immune to it. Nobody out here has ever played perfectly for even a single round. Think of that." Who but the Scots could have invented a game like this?

Jimmy Demaret was an uncommon golfer in that he could take the game but rarely himself seriously. Laughs and the companionship of his pals ranked high, as did women and music and an occasional libation. Almost any occasion. Jimmy learned his best golf on the windswept flats of east Texas where he discovered what the wind was good for. A man who could make the wind work for him, he found, was apt to collect plenty of loose change.

James Newton Demaret became one of the best wind players of his or any other day and won over thirty official PGA tournaments, including three Masters. He was among the best players in an era that produced a pack of legends, but as amiable and as good as Demaret and his generation were, none was above getting his comeuppance. In one tournament, Jimmy came to the last hole leading by two strokes, but in a frightful lapse he knocked four balls out-of-bounds. He was paired with Lew Worsham, he of the lantern jaw and the quick needle. "For your information," Worsham dryly observed, "you're shooting nine."

Why should we repeat this story about one of our favorite people? For one thing, these fellows were not out for smiles on a summer afternoon. They wanted to beat an opponent's brains out and when they got him on the ground, as Snead would tell anyone, to stomp him again until nothing was left—nothing that could hurt you, anyway. That sounds particularly bloodthirsty to us today, but that's the way it was. And the pros had good reasons, too; there wasn't enough money to go around, and they were scrapping for meager purses. Unlike today, the top dog always collected most of the prize money, and the rest of the crowd ate stale bread and oranges. But this time Demaret, one of the top dogs and a straight driver, at that, simply had lost it at the last hole. Could there be a clearer reminder of how fickle and humbling the game can be?

Maybe. His pal Ben Hogan had finally won a tournament, the 1940 North and South Open, after struggling for ten years with an unruly swing. Then, following World War II, Hogan won his first major, the 1946 PGA Championship at Portland Golf Club in Oregon. That same year he finished a stroke behind the winner at both the Masters and the U. S. Open, so as the 1947 season got underway, he had a renewed confidence and reasons to feel that his time had arrived. In the Jacksonville Open, Ben started well but, at the short sixth, dunked his tee shot into a shallow pond that fronted the green. Water barely covered his ball, so Hogan tried to splash it onto dry land. Four times his club ripped into the water without much effect, so Ben lifted and dropped. With the penalty, he was lying six. A poor pitch found the water again, and again he lifted and dropped. Ben made the green with his ninth stroke and two-putted for his eleven. This is so uncharacteristic of the Hogan we've heard about, and yet so typical of the game.

Clayton Heafner was a contemporary of Hogan's and Demaret's, a burly redhead from North Carolina who was twice runner-up in the U. S. Open and occasionally was described as the angriest man in golf. He is also believed to be the last American pro to be laid a stymie in competition, which happened in a 1951 Ryder Cup match with Irishman Fred Daly; the stymie was outlawed six weeks later. Heafner didn't suffer fools. He was having a difficult time in one tournament, sprayed a few shots into the woods, and finally told his caddie he was picking up. An old lady in the gallery piped up: "You get right back there and play that ball, Mr. Heafner! I bought you in the betting pool." Clayton glanced up, handed her his club, and said: "Okay, lady, you play the sunovabitch," turned around and walked to the clubhouse. He had a temper to go with his talent, but he also understood how fickle the game is, and accepted it. In a U. S. Open, Heafner walked off the eighteenth green looking glum after posting a 72. The veteran Jock Hutchison was standing there, and exclaimed: "A 72! That can't be, Clayt; you went out in 32." Heafner didn't even smile: "Yeah, but I had to come back." So must they all.

Old-timers may recall Bob Panasiuk, a fine Canadian player who compiled a respectable record on both the Canadian and U. S. tours. Bob is the youngest player to make the cut in a PGA Tour event, the Canadian Open, at the age of fifteen years, eight months, younger even than Ty Tryon. Tryon made the cut in Orlando in 2001 at sixteen (tall, long-hitting Michelle Wie at age fourteen came within a stroke of making the cut in the 2004 Hawaiian Open, barely missing lowering the age mark and also becoming the first woman to make a cut on the men's tour). In the 1965 U. S. Open, at Bellerive in St. Louis, Panasiuk knocked his tee shot to within twenty feet of the cup at the sixth, another of those pesky par-threes with a pond in front. All seemed safe until he putted; a sudden twitch, and the ball was away, darting across the green into the water. His mind blanked; Panasiuk dropped a ball *on the other side of the pond* when he had every right to take a penalty stroke and replay the putt from his spot on the green. Before anyone realized what was happening, he had dumped two more shots into the water. The poor man finally made the green in seven, after having reached it in one a quarter of an hour earlier, and had two putts for a nine.

Brian Barnes, the giant Scot who usually played with a pipe clenched between his considerable double-row of choppers, was a mighty hitter and fierce competitor like most of his race. While not the greatest of putters, Barnes made up for it with bravery and get-along. The brawny Scot played two famous Ryder Cup matches with Nicklaus, when Jack was more or less in his prime. Barnes was never going to be the loser and won many hearts, including Jack's own.

In the second round of the 1968 French Open at Saint Cloud, Barnes bunkered his tee shot at the par-three eighth hole. After a mediocre stroke from the sand, Barnes left his long putt short, then missed the next. Peter Dobereiner described what followed: "With that old red curtain coming down over his eyes, he raked at the ball and missed, and now he was lost. He patted the ball to and fro and by the time it dropped, what with penalty strokes for hitting a moving ball and standing astride the line, his playing

Brian Barnes was a mighty player and sportsman, capable of glorious victory over Jack Nicklaus one day and ignominious defeat at the hands of his own putter the next.

partners reckoned him down in fifteen strokes." Following the wreckage, Barnes swiftly departed the scene and was seen no more that day.

Competing in the British Open at The Old Course in St. Andrews, Scotland, Barnes's old rival Jack Nicklaus found Hell Bunker, the same pit that had swallowed Sarazen's hopes for victory in 1933. This particular depravity has steep, vertical sides fashioned from stacked bricks of turf that rise about six feet all the way around. Not a very nice place to be if you are in the hunt in the world's most venerable championship. Jack took five to escape the pit, and marked an eleven on his card. Sarazen was not the first nor will Nicklaus be the last to be humbled by this well-named hazard. On another day, Jack posted an 80 in competition; not in a Senior PGA tournament, mind you, but in a regular tour event. Playing in the Masters, he came to the Augusta National's twelfth, that tiny scorpion of a par-three. Watching from a golf cart nearby was the club's founder, Bob Jones. Nicklaus shanked his tee shot, and no more need be said. If Jack Nicklaus could suffer these humiliations at the careless hands of golf, who are we to complain when the game treats one of us rudely?

Cary Middlecoff came on tour in 1946, fresh out of the U. S. Army and a hot amateur career in which he had distinguished himself by winning one of the PGA Tour's prestigious events, the 1945 North and South Open. Grouped the last two rounds with Ben Hogan and Gene Sarazen, the brash amateur won by five strokes.

"I didn't think anybody could beat me," he said.

None of those phenoms ever does. Purses were small in those days, and the pros had learned the fine art of staging exhibition matches to supplement their incomes. A promotion-minded sports reporter of the *Memphis Commercial Appeal* named Early Maxwell organized a series of matches between Middlecoff, the hometown hero, and Sam Snead, a fellow southerner who, next to Byron Nelson, was the game's biggest draw.

Following the custom of the time, tickets were sold to all comers and the receipts shared among the promoter and players. Early Maxwell offered Snead the choice of a $500 guarantee per match

Cary "Doc" Middlecoff (left) was a brash amateur when he challenged the famous pro, Sam Snead (right), in an exhibition match. Given a choice, Sam took the cash guarantee and lived to regret it.

or a share of the split. Five hundred bucks bought a lot of groceries in 1945, and Sam, always careful with cash, took the guarantee. Off they went to play the first scheduled match in Louisville, Kentucky. The day dawned sunny and warm and the match drew 12,000 fans. "Early and I made $11,000 apiece," said Middlecoff. "Sam was so busy counting the gallery he got to where he couldn't play a lick. It just killed him all the money we were making." Winners and losers.

Middlecoff was a tall, lanky native of Memphis with a pleasant drawl, an easy manner, and a keen intellect. He had earned a degree in dentistry, which he practiced briefly in the Army before seeking the lusher pastures of professional golf, and later wrote several books on the fine points of golf instruction. He was also as nervous as a hen in a bare barnyard which led to deliberate, sometimes agonizingly slow habits on the golf course. But Doc could play, as they say. He was very long and very straight with his driver and all the irons save one. His only weakness was playing a sand iron. By professional standards, he was more or less pathetic. But he didn't get in many bunkers, and you wouldn't want to try him on the green because he could putt with anybody. Middlecoff was as likely to hole a twenty-footer as a two-footer, and his fellow pros knew it. A warm and genial man off the course, Doc was occasionally temperamental on it.

In 1953 Middlecoff was approaching his peak. He had won the 1949 U. S. Open at Chicago's rugged Medinah #3 and was competing in another at Oakmont Country Club in Pennsylvania, its bunkers still furrowed by those evil, wide-tined rakes devised by Henry Fownes. For the fourth consecutive year Doc had drawn an afternoon starting time. This irritated him. He had only himself to blame, of course, because leading contenders were often given late starting times to attract spectators and Cary had been in contention every year since he won the Open. Middlecoff played the first nine in good order, but the late starting time continued to weigh on his mind. At the tenth hole, he hit his second into a greenside bunker. The green sits close beside the Pennsylvania Turnpike, which cuts through the Oakmont property. As he moved into the bunker, the annoyance ripening, Middlecoff looked down at the ball and suddenly it came to him: "You don't have to take this anymore," he told himself.

Who can doubt that the game is animated by wicked impulses? Instead of the soft explosion that everyone was expecting, Cary

Middlecoff took a deliberate, full-blooded, menacing swing. The ball soared over the trees guarding the boundary of the property and crashed into the Pennsylvania Turnpike. In the U. S. By-God Open! His startled playing partner, Walter Burkemo, would never forget it. "It went into the turnpike like a flaming dart," Burkemo reported with his customary deadpan expression, although "flaming" was not exactly the word he used. There were rumors that the club followed it, whirling majestically over the trees like a disembodied helicopter blade, but Middlecoff denied it. Without a word, he turned and walked in. "I must not have been in a very good humor," Cary said later. "I'm sorry I did it, but I've done lots of things I'm sorry about."

What more need be said of a game that had one of the greatest players in the world in its grasp and had rendered him helpless? Golf seems so well conceived to humble us. Bernard Darwin once explained that in each golfer dwells an element of Hyde with Jekyll, and that we constantly battle the two. "Even in the greatest golfers," said Darwin, "the fiend lurks," citing the example of James Braid, a long hitter and the most stoic of men: "Once in a great while, in the exuberance of the blow when he hits a stupendous hook into the heather, do we not catch a glimpse beneath that angelic exterior of the simian Hyde? And is there not, my fellow sinners, just a grain of comfort in that?"

So there we are in our envy and spite, for all to see. Darwin was himself a fiercely partisan competitor who admitted that he could not help secretly rooting for an opponent's demise, nor did he wish to deprive himself of this pleasure. Most of us are like that, and when the match doesn't go our way we are apt to grow irritable or, if nothing else works, to shrug in resignation. The reclusive American humorist Will Cuppy had a comforting phrase to help him through these rough patches, a kind of lament for the perpetually overmatched loser:

"It can't be helped," he would say, and move on. Not that this would be a very welcome consolation to most of us when a sudden gust carries a shot into the hay or a blade of grass sends a putt wobbling from its line. On the other hand, if we can accept the reality that we are all born losers, in both golf and life, then perhaps we can free our minds enough to enjoy the journey. We might remember that it is we who seek the journey and only once that the destination would seek us.

CHAPTER
SIX

POWER SHANKING

"It's the worst place you have ever been."
—Whitbread sailor, on the Southern Ocean

Ben Hogan's first book, *Power Golf*, hit American golf in 1948 like a rocket. Hogan had won both the Los Angeles and U. S. Opens that year at Riviera, the first of several golf courses to be dubbed "Hogan's Alley" by the press. Hogan controlled Riviera, then as now one of the most admired courses the pros regularly play. He had learned how to do this to golf courses. Ben Hogan was hot. The book was hot. Everyone wanted to know what Hogan knew about the golf swing, never dreaming that behind all that physical stuff was a mind of steel. The book was the idea of Henry Luce, who owned *Time* and *Life* magazines and was so keen to publish it, the story went, that he bankrolled a publishing company, A. S. Barnes, more or less to do so. Luce was said to have paid Hogan a reported $50,000, a lot of money in those days, and the book sold like crazy. What Hogan thought about

Ben Hogan resting at the practice range at Riviera, a course dubbed Hogan's Alley after Ben won both the Los Angeles and U. S. Opens there in 1948. His book, *Power Golf,* came out later that year.

all this is not recorded, except that he couldn't restrain a crooked smile when the fifty grand was mentioned.

It had been in my mind to use the title of this chapter for the book itself in the time-honored custom of riding on another man's popular title, but the publisher would have none of it. "No golfer will touch the thing," he grumbled. Still, I could not resist a perverse impulse in naming this chapter for an affliction that is held in pure terror by almost every golfer, good or bad. So evil is this affliction that golfers won't utter its name.

The shanks. There, we've said it, and we've had it, and it's a poxy, vicious, degrading, horrid, disgusting thing. It leaves men helpless and begging the Almighty to open the heavens and swallow them whole. Strangely, Ben Hogan only once seems to have experienced a case of shanking, but his great contemporary Byron Nelson did.

Contrary to what you may have heard in neighborhood saloons

and caddie pens, shanking is not a laughing matter. To be blunt, it is personal and humiliating. I have seen its effects at first hand. Although the championship, if that's what one can call it, of the Golf Writers' Association of America is hardly the U. S. Open, or even the Gasparillo Invitational, those of us who have contended for this paltry achievement have done so in pursuit of an age-old desire—to club our fellow writers into submission, if only for a short while, and even if under the influence of strong spirits. I mention all this for a reason. In the early 1970s, which is an antebellum period for those not old enough to remember the cash-in putter craze, I watched one of our distressed brethren come to the final hole at the Dunes Golf and Beach Club, a course that is one of Robert Trent Jones's better designs (excepting only one hole) needing a five for 75. I cannot remember if that score would have won the event, but it would have been close and that was enough to tempt fate. It certainly tempted him.

Back in those days, the eighteenth hole at the Dunes course was a short par-five, reachable in two for long hitters, which this fellow imagined himself to be, but whose factual justification is probably open to debate. Since then, the hole has been shortened somewhat, converted into a rather strong par-four requiring a middle to long iron second over a pond to a wide, shallow green. This fellow laid his second shot just short of the water that stretches across the front of the green, a wily play if ever he played one. It must be said that he was at the time suffused in an alcoholic stupor, having consumed an undetermined amount the previous evening along with a ration of hair of the dog that very morning. How he reached the eighteenth in 70 strokes is one of those mysteries golf is full of. These things happen in golf. So does what happened next.

Surveying the approach, this golfer coolly estimated the short distance remaining to the green. A smooth pass with the pitching club would do nicely, he thought. But his eyes kept taking in the broad pond that lay before him and distorted judgment took care of what common sense remained. His hand dove into the golf bag and seized the sand wedge, reasoning no doubt that a crisp shot with the more lofted club might do better in the circumstances and in his alcoholic condition.

Well, you know the rest. He carefully and cold-bloodedly shanked seven balls into the pond, each stroke accompanied by that awful, shuddering vibration at impact that marks the genuine article, the weak, dreaded, muffled clank of hosel meeting ball. Believe me when I tell you that the fellow tried his utmost on every single stroke. Finally, he could take no more, grabbed a wooden club and skipped a low, screaming shot across the water. The ball stuck in the bank behind the green and, after more adventures there, he eventually holed out in twenty-three. I cannot bring myself to name the poor wretch. A year earlier, the legendary Dudley "Waxo" Green, Nashville's silver-tongued golf scribe, had committed a similar indiscretion at this very same hole, although he escaped with only a twelve. No, the twenty-three deserves its infamy, as the legendary New Jersey scribe Red Hoffman reminds this fellow whenever he has the chance.

These were only golf writers, so what else should we expect? True, but if you think the pros are not subject to this kind of indignity, you are mistaken. Remember Philip Walton? The fine Irish pro and mainstay of the European Tour in the 1990s? The same fellow who holed that long putt to clinch the Ryder Cup Matches of 1997? Well, ten years earlier the very same Walton shanked fourteen consecutive shots in a European Tour event held in

Monte Carlo. The poor man nearly gave up the game, and who can blame him?

Why bother to bring up the horrid affliction? It disfigures the game and our very souls, so why pay it the courtesy of mentioning the scurvy thing? Because, dear friends, it visits almost every golfer at one time or another and when it does, it cannot be ignored. If it has spared you, you've probably made a pact with the devil. It comes upon us unbidden, unexpected, day or night, rain or shine, happy or sad, none of that matters. When the thing strikes, there is nothing to do but shudder and hope it will pass.

How then can we explain someone who *deliberately* sets out to shank the ball? To hit one of these unmentionables accidentally is one thing, but to do it on purpose is to brazenly tempt the fates no matter how gifted the golfer. This, as they say, is a true story and it happened on the professional tour during the era when players had personalities. The incident involved two extraordinarily intense fellows who also happened to be cutups when the mood struck them. The first of these was Bob Toski, a mere slip of a man whose frail frame and skinny appendages quickly earned him the nickname "Mouse." The second was Ed "Porky" Oliver, a man whose nickname fairly describes his figure.

That this Mutt and Jeff pair should become great pals seems as natural as any other opposites who attract. Porky Oliver was older and had achieved perhaps more in the game with his near victories in the U. S. Open and the Bing Crosby tournament, while Toski was reckoned a comer despite his 118 pounds. He would later win the World Championship of Golf and with it a cash prize of $100,000, the largest in history up to that time. The Mouse was blessed with superb hand-eye coordination and blinding speed of hand and wrist, all of which had allowed him to become one of the very longest hitters in golf, and pound for pound possibly the longest ever.

Both men were natural entertainers who kept galleries warm with laughter. On this occasion, Pork Chops and Mouse found themselves on the practice range one morning at the Hartford tournament waiting to tee off. To excite the fans, they decided to stage a shanking contest. Now shanking a ball unintentionally is one thing; hitting a deliberate shank requires a refined gift of hand-eye magic. Oliver and Toski each had plenty of that. *Zing*, went one from Toski; *zang* went another from Oliver. They began inventing their own unusual types of shanked shots while the fans howled with delight.

Among those who witnessed this madness was Gardner Dickinson, a close friend of Toski's and one of the pro tour's earnest defenders of decorum and seriousness—he was, after all, a disciple of Hogan's. *Joing* came the dreaded sound as a ball darted across Dickinson's line of flight. *Twang* came another. Although the gallery was falling on the ground in fairly helpless laughter, none of the pros was amused. The gods don't even want to be in the neighborhood when someone is shanking for fear the affliction might be contagious.

After the round was over, Dickinson returned to the locker room. As he began changing his shoes, in came Toski, his face drawn. He slumped into a chair not saying a word, staring at the wall with a glazed expression.

"What's the matter, Blue?" asked Gardner. "Didn't you play well?"

Toski barely shook his head. "No," he moaned, "it was awful."

"What happened?" A long pause.

"There'll be no more of those damn contests," he croaked.

"What do you mean?" asked Dickinson.

"I hit five of those bastards today, that's what I mean," hissed Toski.

Years later, Dickinson chuckled at the memory. "Bob could do anything with a golf ball, and still can, but I don't think he tempted the fates anymore with that little trick. I'm not sure why the shanks stay with you, but I suspect it's mental or emotional. Maybe it's just plain fear; once that fear gets a lock on your brain, it's such a powerful image that you're a gone goose. I'm not sure I should be mentioning it now."

In the professional ranks, there has probably not been a more famous victim than Byron Nelson. He was a tall man of almost six-feet-two, which affected the method he worked out to perfect his swing. For some reason, tall men—those over six feet—seem to be more susceptible to shanking than those under six feet. Cary Middlecoff, who stood a bit over six-foot-two, was another great player who was pestered occasionally by the unmentionables. In such tall men, the natural swing tends to go round the back rather too easily, which carries the club too abruptly inside and forces a compensatory move outward. This move leads the hosel of the club dangerously near to or into the ball. Somewhere I recall hearing that a shank is as close to perfect impact as it's possible to achieve, which may account for why Nelson was an occasional victim. No one, we're told, not even Hogan, hit more perfect iron shots than Byron Nelson.

Nelson believed that a common cause of shanking was to allow the head to move past the ball in the downswing. This action, Nelson confirmed, forces the swing to move more around the body which, in turn, causes the path of the forward swing to move in a sharply in-to-out direction. This is an invitation to shanking even if you have a great pair of hands, as Nelson did. Lord Byron said that Hogan was saved by his head position. In *Shape Your Swing the Modern Way*, written with Larry Dennis,

Byron Nelson was a tall man occasionally pestered by shanking as a young golfer. Byron was a fiercely competitive golfer, like his friend Ben Hogan, but unlike him, a nervous one. Nelson only once recalls Hogan hitting a shank, and thought he never hit another because it frightened him so.

Nelson noted that Ben kept his head as steady as a rock and almost never let it move past the ball during his swing. "I only remember seeing Hogan shank the ball once, and it frightened him because he'd never done it before," Nelson said.

Byron was not so lucky. His upright swing and lanky frame made him a natural target of the virus, a fact that makes his later achievements all the more remarkable. In 1936 Nelson won his first big title, the Metropolitan Open in New York, just four years after he turned pro. Later that summer he went to Pinehurst hoping to qualify for the PGA Championship but he shanked his second shot on the third hole, a nicely-shaped, medium-length par-four, recorded an eight, and failed to qualify for match-play. There would be other visitations, but keeping a steady head, Byron said, helped cure him of this vile tendency.

THE AFFLICTED

The great golf architect Alister Mackenzie was himself a lifelong shanker. In his splendid manuscript, *The Spirit of St. Andrews*, published posthumously by his nephew Raymond Haddock, Mackenzie tells the sad story of Lister Kaye, a fine golfer of the day who reached the final match of the 1919 British Army Championship. Kaye was dormie seven and shanked to lose the hole, said Mackenzie, then continued to shank the rest of the way in and lost the match to Charles Hope. The fear of shanking, according to Mackenzie, haunted the man the rest of his days; a few years later, Kaye had gone from scratch to a twelve handicap. Mackenzie attributed his own shanking to anxiety and a rushed backswing that forced the weight onto his toes. "Slow back while keeping your eye on the ball is no remedy, either; in fact, they

The persistence of shanking has troubled many famous persons, including the golf architect Alister Mackenzie (above) who eventually was cured by the English teacher, Ernest Jones.

make it worse," Mackenzie said in the book. Ernest Jones, the famous one-legged teacher, finally cured Mackenzie by having him complete the wrist cock before starting his downswing. Is this a reliable cure for shanking? Who knows? Its arrival is as mysterious as its departure. In his memoir, Mackenzie also claimed that J. H. Taylor suffered from shanking for two years and gave up the game for a whole year because of it, but he gives no other details. Taylor, perhaps understandably, never mentioned the subject in his books.

As Mackenzie and Dickinson hinted, it may be the fear of it that keeps haunting those of us who have been so rudely visited. Paul Azinger admitted to this fear and its affects on his performance at Doral one year. Needing a par at the last to win, Azinger bogeyed and lost in a playoff. He told writer Tim Rosaforte afterward that he had not been confident over the ball all week, afraid he might shank. It got so bad that before Sunday's round he took a basket of balls to an adjacent course and hit seven-irons for two hours, trying to convince himself that his swing would hold up. "I never felt comfortable all week. As awful as I felt over the ball, I should have been glad to be in that position, but felt like I was choking. Golf is really a head game."

Of course it is, and it takes a character with rough bark to shake off the demons. In the 1932 British Open, held at Prince's Golf Club, in Sandwich, England, Gene Sarazen set the place on fire with three rounds in the sixties. After three easy pars to start the fourth round, Gene shanked his approach to the fourth hole, startling everyone, including his caddie, an aging Skip Daniels. Henry Longhurst confessed to a fondness for Daniels's response as he replaced the club in Sarazen's bag. Said the old caddie: "I don't think we shall be requiring that one again, sir." No indeed, and Sarazen finished, as Jones said, in a parade to add—after a decade of trying—the British Open to his glittering list of American conquests. Bobby Jones claimed he never shanked in his life, but in one of his books felt obliged to offer a cure. He wrote rather gingerly: "I know that the evil is cumulative and lives upon itself. For that reason, I advise golfers who never have shanked to read no further. It is a thing to cure but not something to think about preventing." Does this comment have a certain defensive edge to it? Can we be sure that Jones never shanked?

OTHER VICTIMS

In 1921 Jim Barnes scored an impressive victory in the U. S. Open, held at Columbia Country Club in Maryland, finishing eight strokes ahead of Walter Hagen and Fred McLeod. Barnes was a tall, lean native of Cornwall, England, who had emigrated to the U. S., where he won the first PGA Championship in 1916. So the fellow could play, but in the PGA Championship of 1924, held at French Lick, Indiana, the dreadful, unexpected visitor ended his hopes of another PGA. Barnes came to the last hole of the thirty-six-hole final against Hagen with a chance to send the match to extra holes, but he shanked his approach and allowed Hagen to win the second of his four consecutive PGA Championships. Known as Long Jim, for both his height and the length of his tee shots, Barnes would go on to win the British Open at Prestwick in 1925. He was said to be a quiet, methodical golfer not openly subject to the sudden moods and twitches of a more temperamental nature, which only confirms that the affliction can strike anyone.

Johnny Miller is another tall fellow who had an occasional bout with the shanks. His most famous happened on the sixteenth hole at Pebble Beach during the final round of the Bing Crosby Pro-Am. Miller was bidding to win as he stepped into his iron approach to the slanting green. The ball darted to the right with that shuddering sound no player wants to hear, and finished among the bushes and trees, alongside Miller's hopes for victory.

One can so easily sympathize with these fellows. Colin Montgomerie had been frustrated in his attempts to win the British Open for so many years, but in 2002 at Muirfield in his native Scotland, Colin had played a sensational second round of 64 to climb into contention. Perhaps this would be his year. But the fates were not kind. Early in that dreadful third round, when the winds and rain

Long Jim Barnes had his bouts with shanking, but unlike Byron Nelson he was a quiet, methodical player not given to nervous moods or bouts of fierceness, which just proves that the virus can strike anyone.

smashed even the great Tiger Woods into mediocrity, Montgomerie drove a tee shot into the tall fescue hay on the left side of the long fifth hole, then shanked his second across the fairway into the equally gnarly stuff on the right side, a perfectly understandable mishap considering the horrid conditions. A double-bogey there began a dreadful slide to a round of 84, and hopes smothered once again. Curtis Strange, safe in his television booth, commented that in foul weather he, too, had always had a tendency to shank because of an urge to move down into the shot. That seems to be a fairly common source of the calamity and a pattern worth guarding against.

SOME FAMOUS CURES

The history of golf is full of similar horror stories, usually embellished by our terror over the possibility of another sudden attack, and many theories have been proposed to explain the causes of shanking. Less publicized are the attempted cures for the very

Colin Montgomerie had full sails furled in the high winds at Muirfield at the 2002 Open Championship, but a wayward tee shot early in the third round was followed by a startling shank from deep rough, smothering his hopes and leading to a fatal slide.

good reason that few people are willing to leap in and confront a deadly snake. A noted exception is the cure developed by Jack Burke Jr. early in his career. After serving an apprenticeship under Claude Harmon at Winged Foot in Mamaroneck, New York, Burke took the head pro's job at Metropolis Country Club in nearby White Plains. Metropolis has a fine heritage of first-class professionals that includes Paul Runyan, Harry Cooper, Burke, and later

Not every golf pro is anxious to attempt to cure a golfer of a shanking problem, but Jack Burke Jr. stumbled on a method that seems to work. Other pros and characters proclaim their own cures nearby.

on, Gene Borek. One of the members had developed a curious variation of the shanks. "He didn't shank the ball out in the fairway; only when he got close to the green would the affliction appear," said Burke. "He had it so bad sometimes that he couldn't get that old U. S. Royal on the putting surface. He kept shanking the ball all the way around the edge of the green until you had to laugh or cry at the guy's misery."

This pathetic scene, apparently repeated week in and week out, led fellow members to make a standing offer of $500 to any pro who could get the man out of his rut. Eventually Burke found an answer. "I'd lay awake nights trying to figure out a cure for this poor soul," said Burke. "He was a pipe smoker, and always had an expensive pipe he treated like a baby. One day, I put that pipe along the line of play on the other side of his golf ball and told him to hit the ball. If he shanked, he was gonna smash the club into his favorite pipe and obliterate it." Swinging gingerly, the man hit the ball gently on the toe of the club and chipped it beautifully. From that day on, he always laid his pipe alongside the ball and reportedly never shanked again.

But that's not the end of the story. As everyone in golf must know, the same Jack Burke and his friend Jimmy Demaret partnered to build Champions Golf Club in Houston, which boasts two of the best golf courses in Texas, and a membership of hard-core golfers. Burke was telling this story of the pipe one day at Champions when a member overheard it, went off and didn't return for about an hour. He walked back to the group with his arms outstretched, his pipe in pieces, and proclaimed: "Jackie, I just came from the range and that deal don't work for three-irons!"

Ted Kroll, a fine player of the 1950s and 1960s, played lots of golf with Burke, from whom he may have picked up the idea. Kroll's variation was more draconian, however. For golfers afflicted with chronic shanking on full shots, Kroll would ask for the fellow's wrist watch—the more expensive the better—and lay it down just outside the ball parallel to the line of the swing. "Go ahead and take a rip," Kroll would exhort. "If you shank it, there goes your Rolex!"

JoAnne Carner, one of the greatest woman golfers, was a notorious shanker. "In the early 1970s, I had a terrible case of the shanks," Carner said. "I'd come into the locker room before a round, and before the other girls knew I was there, I'd hear someone say, 'Oh no, I'm paired with Carner today. I'll catch the shanks from her for sure.' Nice way to start the round." Her Florida neighbor, Gardner Dickinson, came to the rescue. Carner says she sometimes fell into the habit of bending over too far as she waggled. "That caused me to go forward as I swung, so Gardner told me to sit back on my heels and stand tall. He got me out of it."

John Jacobs, as he usually did, diagnosed the problem using simple geometry and applied an equally simple correction: "One cause of shanking is playing the ball too far forward, which usually opens the shoulders, as well. The swing, which tends to follow the shoulder line, then goes too far round the back and returns outward, which leads the hosel into the ball. To correct this, play the ball farther back in your stance and square your shoulders so that you can swing the club up and down along the correct path from the inside into the back of the ball and back inside again." Not too far inside, though. Chuck Cook, the fine teacher from Austin, Texas, has noticed that golfers who swing too quickly inside, especially on chip shots, run the risk of shanking because it makes their swings too shallow. This gets the clubhead swinging very close to the ground and tends to push the whole business out toward the target line as contact approaches, and there the little darling is.

CURES OFFERED BY VARIOUS CRACKS AND CRANKS

Here are additional pearls offered by some of the game's bolder pundits:

Lee Trevino: "Make sure your right knee can clear under your hands at address and you'll be okay." Say what?

Roger Maltbie, to writer Dan Jenkins: "Try to hit it left." Jenkins said this cured him of shanking, but then he needed a cure for hitting shots to the left.

Gardner Dickinson: "The common denominator in shanking is that the shoulders at impact have dropped considerably lower than they were at address; the arms fold and block the swing, so the heel of the club leads the clubface into the ball. The cure? Keep the head up!"

Sam Snead: "The end cause of shanking is that the club moves too far beyond its correct path in the downswing and by the time it gets to the ball, you're cooked. The reason is that the shaft is laid off and points behind you. The best cure I know is to cock the wrists so that the shaft points straight up at the top of the swing, and that way it can swing downward instead of outward."

David Leadbetter: "Make the hands swing closer to the body."

Bob Toski: "Most shankers I see are hand-wrist players with tremendous finger tension. To cure these folks, I tee up the ball and tell them to hold the club as lightly as possible, then swing smoothly, letting the clubface open during the backswing and close in the downswing with its own momentum."

Jack Lemmon: "Try poking yourself in the eye with a sharp stick; anything is better than hitting another one of those things!"

Peter Kostis: "Huh?"

Cary Middlecoff: "The primary cause of shanking is when golfers move toward the ball during the forward swing, so I advise keeping the weight on the heels."

Paul Runyan: "The shank is golf's Black Death. It feeds on itself because of a buildup of tension that causes golfers to grip tighter and tighter. Loosen your grip, swing more upright, and cup your left wrist as you swing back. This will encourage a more vertical downswing and less tension as you meet the ball."

William Shakespeare: "What hast thou said? Yon's the ugliest word I've ever heard."

The eminent British writer Bernard Darwin (above) announced that he had found a cure for shanking, invented by Englishman Charles Hutchings. Darwin treated the subject with sufficient delicacy that one can easily imagine him having been, at times, a victim.

Harvey Penick: "Feel like the toe of the club is rolling over. It's almost impossible to hit a 'lateral' if the blade is closed. Try it sometime."

J. H. Taylor: "Induce the left arm to graze the coat both going up and coming down; that way the right arm cannot stray or push the club outward." Well, I suppose almost anything is worth a try.

Bernard Darwin weighed in on the subject, then called "socketing," about a hundred years ago, claiming to have pried the cure from Charles Hutchings who did not take up golf until he was over thirty and achieved fame for winning the British Amateur Championship at the age of fifty-three. Hutchings is the man Darwin credits with coining the phrase: "Golf is nine-tenths mental." Hutchings's cure: "Rip the club right through with the right hand." That's all there is to his advice, although it goes against much of conventional teaching both then and now. "I cannot reconcile the two points of view," said Darwin. " I can only state that I believe Hutchings to be right, and others wrong."

Charles Hutchings may have been encouraging victims to "release" the club as they swing through, which can only occur when the golfer allows enough room between player and ball for the arms and club to pass easily and without interference, something alluded to in an earlier chapter. When golfers try to control the ball too much, or develop anxieties about a critical shot, tensions rise and muscles tighten. We dip and jerk and lunge as we swing. Flubs and shanks are not uncommon results. Although it may seem out of place to say so here, one of the ironies of golf lies in learning to control our swings less to obtain more in the way of golf shots that make us happy. Anyone who has taken lessons from John Jacobs may remember his saying time and again that

DE-control, not control is the goal, and perhaps even a secret, of consistent golf.

It is only a conjecture on my part, but I've often wondered if Ben Hogan didn't eventually come to understand and embrace this principle. It is true that when the young Hogan released his swing, most of the time the ball hooked, often very sharply. As he persevered, he grew to understand what he himself must do to straighten his shots. Distance was vital to a man of his comparatively small stature and he must have figured out that achieving a free release not only meant greater distance, but straighter shots. He would have seen this in players like Bobby Jones, Sam Snead, and Bill Mehlhorn, whose swing he openly admired. Instinct is one thing, intelligence another, and Hogan was by contemporary accounts one of the brightest of his profession.

Ben's determination to find an answer to his swing and his willingness to make adjustments led to that extraordinary swing we can see only on film and video nowadays. When Hogan fully released his swing, which in his prime was on almost every shot, the club seemed to travel along the line of play longer than happened with other golfers. Hogan's action carried the club distinctly upwards, rather than around, in a wide, sweeping arc after the ball had been struck. One player today whose follow-through looks a little like this is Vijay Singh, though his rhythm is quite different from Hogan's. In Singh as in Hogan that free and easy forward swing is the mark of an uncontrolled release and is the secret to much of the power and accuracy seen in both players when at the top of their form. In each case it's evident that the unusually high finish is a result of releasing the club along the line of play; that's physics. If you worry that this digresses too far from shanking and its causes, perhaps it does, but it goes back to

When Ben Hogan (left) fully released the club during his swing, it traveled distinctly upwards in a high, sweeping arc that became a noticeable feature of his swing. Vijay Singh (right) is a modern player who exhibits the same trait, a mark of complete release and power.

one of the more useful notions in golf, mentioned earlier, which is yet another antidote to shanking: If we leave room to swing, the club will find the ball, and with no interference, the swing will have every reason to release the club.

However, we can't dwell on such fields of glory when the subject is shanking. Notwithstanding what you have read here, the shank itself will have the last word. The affliction reminds us of Henry Longhurst's description of the yips: "If you've had 'em, you've got 'em, and that's an end on it!" Listen to the sound of it: "Shank!" There is in the word a sibilant suggestion of a snake coiled to strike, that and the harsh sound of iron striking iron with a clank! Then comes the shuddering aftershock. The feeling is even more repugnant than the sound, I am told, and once upon the victim, the sickness clings relentlessly. And then, in Darwin's forlorn phrase, "the waters of bitterness close over our heads."

CHAPTER SEVEN

THE OTHER GAME

"If I made every putt the rest of my life, I still wouldn't be even."
—Tommy Bolt

Putting is a business entirely apart from the rest of golf, which is why some of the great ball strikers began referring to this little stroke rather disdainfully as "The Other Game." The phrase dates back at least to 1905 and Vardon's book *The Complete Golfer*, in which he described putting as "a game within another game," and has been a popular refrain since. Ben Hogan famously wanted to eliminate the hole from golf entirely, telling sports writers at the Masters one year that the game would be so much better if they could only play to flagsticks, and the closest ball would win. Better for Hogan, of course. On the other hand, George Low Jr. gave up the rest of the game altogether to concentrate solely on putting. Low achieved a certain notoriety in 1945 as the man who ended Byron Nelson's streak of consecutive victories at eleven

155

when he claimed the winner's check in Memphis. George didn't win the tournament—an amateur named Fred Haas Jr. did; ironically, Low tied another amateur, Bob Cochran, for second but, as a professional, he collected the money by finishing ahead of Nelson.

George Low had a nose for collecting money. He was the son of a Scottish professional of the same name who came to the United States and settled at Baltusrol, New Jersey, where he became a well-known and accomplished club professional. George Jr. had all the advantages of genes and early training, but he was not a man to exert himself when other means were at hand. He was also rather good at putting. He developed a technique that built on the "gate" idea of Douglas Edgar, an early twentieth-century English professional who had envisioned a golf stroke in which the clubhead moves through an imaginary gate to perfection. The idea was later embellished and adapted for putting by Pembroke A. Vaile, who wrote several books on the subject in the 1920s.

In George Low's method, the gate became something like a door swinging on its hinges. He not only taught putting, he hustled his clients, some of them the game's best-known players with names like Palmer and Rosburg. Low could beat just about anyone, using any putter; he could even beat you putting with his shoe. His ideas on putting were eventually published in a book written with Al Barkow, but George always knew that putting was not a skill that could be conferred; it was born into a few lucky pairs of hands, including his own.

When it comes to putting, we ought to listen to geniuses like George Low, Bobby Locke, Billy Casper, Jerry Barber, Dave Stockton, and Ben Crenshaw. Those fellows never lost it, not even in their dotage. I recall Locke's appearance at a tournament in Indian Wells, California in 1981 when the jowly South African was sixty-four and could barely hit his banana hook much farther than 180 yards, yet he was holing his putts like a teenager.

"I treat a twenty-foot putt or a forty-footer the same as a four-footer," Locke told us with a perfectly straight face. He did, too. Barber and Casper the same. With the possible exceptions of Walter Hagen and the implacable Jerry Travers, those twin terrors of the 1910s and 1920s, could anyone break a rival's will quicker than those two?

Casper was an impassive killer with the blade in his hands, and it was beautiful to watch—square stance, solid as Sunday, a smooth, wristy pop, and a

It is surprising how few pros copied Billy Casper's putting style because no one was better. Maybe it was because few were blessed with his touch and feel, an ability to tap the ball precisely as hard as needed to reach the hole.

satiny roll. Barber's treatment of his fellow pros, by contrast, was a horrid thing to see. He putted with an ungainly, disfigured lump of brass attached to a distinctly upright shaft. Jerry stood about five-feet-six, had bad eyes, and with his rather scrawny frame could not hit the ball very far. Nor sometimes very straight, either. A famous example of his wizardry, which I described in an earlier book, is worth repeating. It occurred at the 1961 PGA Championship at Olympia Fields, a rugged test on the south side of Chicago. Barber was forty-five then, and not listed among the favorites. All the big guns were there—Arnold Palmer, Julius Boros, Open Champion Gene Littler, Doug Ford, Bob Rosburg, Billy Casper, and Gary Player. But the man playing best of all that week was Don January, a slim Texan with a slow gait and a slashing swing. Off the course January was an amiable man, enormously popular with his fellows, with a dry but wicked sense of humor. On the course, he was a hard customer with the approximate disposition of a gunfighter.

The pairings for the final round sent out January with fellow-Texan Ernie Vossler and the undersized but combative Jerry Barber, who frequently looked as if he were playing in a different group. On the third hole, Barber drove into a tree, hit it out left-handed, knocked a four-wood short of the green, and pitched into the hole. Mark down a par-four. Always tenacious, Barber topped his drive at the tenth, hit two more shots, then chipped in from the heavy grass. Another par.

January meanwhile was playing glorious shots, long and accurate, and had built a lead of five strokes. Reaching the eleventh hole, a par-three, he played a majestic stroke that flew straight at the hole, hit the flagstick, and ricocheted into a bunker. Playing next, Barber pulled his ball into a tree and hit a branch; the ball rattled out and onto the green three feet from the hole. A birdie, thank you very much, and a stroke gained. "I was playing like hell, good enough to beat all those guys," January recalled, taking no pleasure in the retelling. The words came from the corner of his mouth, teeth clenched: "I'm four or five shots ahead of him all day long and he keeps pulling stuff like that." It would get worse.

Jerry Barber stood 5-feet-6, wore thick glasses, couldn't see well nor hit the ball very far. He was an absolutely phenomenal golfer, and if not the greatest putter in history, he is certainly among them.

January finally made a bogey at sixteen while Barber serenely holed a putt of twenty-five feet for his birdie. Now two strokes separated the two. It was after seven p.m. and in waning light, Barber changed from dark to light glasses before hitting his tee shot on seventeen. His driver bounced nearly a foot behind the tee peg and his ball ducked into the rough about 130 yards ahead. Another mediocre stroke, and then a nine-iron, pulled badly, came to rest forty feet from the hole. January hit three gorgeous shots—a drive, a three-iron that covered the flag but went just too far and a gallant chip back that nearly fell in. "I don't know how Don's ball stayed out," Barber said sweetly. Just as sweetly, Jerry's long putt with six inches of left-to-right break, dropped in, and so it was on to the eighteenth, a par-four of 436 yards, with Barber still two strokes behind.

January hooked his drive into a fairway bunker and took two more to reach the green. Barber was on in two, but his ball lay roughly sixty feet from the hole across a ledge that ran diagonally between ball and cup. "I was thinking of nothing but holing that putt," said Barber. The ball rolled on, climbing the ledge then swerved to the right, hunting the hole. Leaning on their putters, January and Vossler watched as it rolled on and on. And in. Ken Venturi, who had finished ahead of this group, looked at Barber's position on the last green before turning to walk into the clubhouse when the roar rolled across the grounds.

Don January hit long, beautiful shots with wood and iron, was a good putter, and had a perfect disposition for winning golf—mean and unrelenting. That Jerry Barber would have a chance against such a player seemed unlikely.

"I knew exactly what had happened," said Venturi, shaking his head. "You could drop your whole practice bag down and you couldn't make that putt."

Needing a fourteen-footer to win, January was mortally wounded now: "I had him by two shots and figured a five on this hole would beat him. After that putt of his there wasn't a prayer of making mine, and I didn't." In the playoff, January shot 68 but "the little so-and-so beat me by a stroke."

Barber had made up four strokes in three holes with putts of roughly twenty, forty, and sixty feet, none more improbable than the last. Nothing like it had been seen since the previous century when Willie Park roamed the links, and certainly not in a ma-

Jerry Barber putted with an ungainly lump of brass fastened at the end of a very upright shaft, a club so heavy few others could use it. How he managed the deed is a mystery to this day.

jor championship until Ben Crenshaw's wriggling snakes disappeared down those tiny holes on Augusta's rolling greens in 1984, or those two days in 1966 when Casper's blade brought Palmer and Olympic to heel in that wildest of U. S. Open finishes. Everyone talks about Palmer's collapse, and so it was, but have we forgotten how cold-bloodedly Casper holed a dozen winning or halving putts over those last twenty-seven holes, strokes that simply broke Arnold's great will?

Listening to any of these fellows is instructive, but I suppose my favorite treatise on putting is one of the earliest, the one written by Harry Vardon in his first book. Vardon must have been a player in ten million. He was the paradigm of golf at the turn of the twentieth century, a combination of Sam Snead and Ben Hogan, and like them in his later days, afflicted with what Vardon called "The Jumps." In modern parlance, "The Yips," the uncontrollable twitches that drive so many of the great players from the competitive game. In a minor key, Palmer and Watson—two of the greatest putters our eyes have seen—were similarly afflicted as they moved into their forties and, though not quite the pathetic figures on the green that Vardon and Hogan became, were never the same again.

At first glance, Harry Vardon seems an unlikely source for advice on this subject, but when you think about it, who would know more about the failures and pitfalls of putting than this man, who was one of its most famous victims? Besides, Vardon spoke plainly, and with an admirable blend of intelligence and common sense. "Putting is a delicate matter, and I, of all people, ought to write about it in a delicate way," Vardon said rather gingerly. He went on to say that those who had observed his "infinite capacity for missing little putts" might think him presumptuous to offer instruction. But his words find their marks.

Vardon was convinced that "no amount of teaching will make a golfer hole out long putts with any frequency, nor will it even make him at all certain of getting the short ones down." Experience counts for a great deal in golf, Vardon said, but even that valuable commodity "counts for less in putting than in any other department of the game. Do we not from time to time see beginners who have been on the links but a single month laying their long putts as dead as anybody could wish and getting an amazing percentage of them into the tin itself?" How can this be? Vardon asks himself. "Perhaps their minds are not embarrassed by a knowledge of all the difficulties the ball will meet on its passage from club to hole. They are not afraid of the hole."

Vardon leveled his gaze on the keys to putting more or less indirectly: "For the proper playing of the other strokes in golf, I have told my readers how they should stand and where to put

Harry Vardon as a young man showing off the Laidley grip that, owing to his fame, became known as Vardon's grip. Putting was not the best part of Harry's game, although he studied it with the greatest care, and his words ring true.

their feet. I have no similar instruction to offer in the matter of putting. There is no rule, and there is no best way. There is more individuality in putting than in any other department of golf, and it is absolutely imperative that this individuality should be allowed to have its way. I believe that every man has had a particular kind of putting method awarded to him by Nature, and when he puts exactly in this way he will do well, and when he departs from his natural he will miss the long ones and the short ones too." No one has put it more plainly.

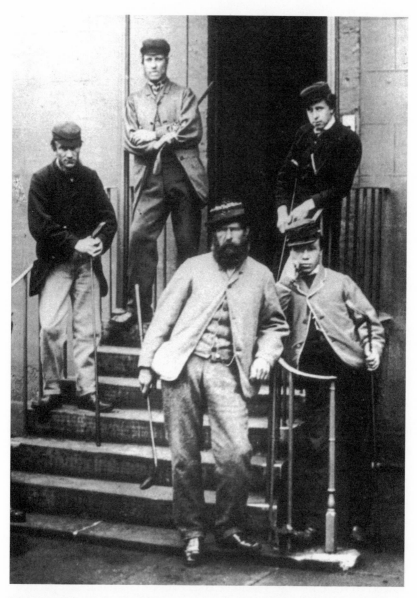

Masters of the game in 1867 surround Old Tom Morris (foreground) who had just won his fourth Open Championship at Prestwick; they are (L-R) David Park, Willie Dunn Sr., Young Tom Morris, and Bob Kirk. The following year, Young Tom, 17, who wickedly chided his father for timid putting, returned and won the first of four straight championships.

Vardon was a great believer in "never up, never in." "The hole will never come to you; let it be an invariable practice to play for the back of the tin so that you will always have just a little in hand. One of the greatest worries of Old Tom Morris was that for a long time in the middle of his career he was nearly always short with his long putts, and his son, Young Tom, wickedly used to say that his father would be a great putter if the hole were only a yard nearer. Tom was conscious of his failing and made strenuous efforts to correct it, and only shows what a terrible habit being short can become, and what necessity there is for the golfer to establish the practice of being up every time. Often enough he will run over, but sometimes the kind hole will gobble the ball, and on the average he will gain substantially over the nervous, hesitating player who is always short."

Bobby Jones, on the other hand, was a man to "die them in the hole" and incomparably the better putter, which might tempt us to listen more closely to his advice. He claimed that putts traveling slowly are greeted by a full-sized cup while fast-moving putts shrink the hole by an inch or so. Bold putters have learned, incidentally, that they can straighten many of the tricky breaks in a green by stroking more firmly. This has been part of golfing lore since Walter Simpson in 1887. Many examples include Hagen and Palmer in the last century and Mickelson in this one. However, many of those who live by that sword are apt to die by it, too.

To those golfers who agree with his admonition about seeking the putting stance Nature ordains, Harry Vardon offered this suggestion: "When they are fairly on their putting, and are apparently doing all that Nature intended and are feeling contented in body and mind, they should take a sly but very careful look at their feet and body and everything else just after they have made a successful long putt, having felt certain all the time that they would make it. This examination should not be premeditated because that would probably spoil the whole thing; and it usually happens that the golfer is too carried away by his emotions of delight to engage in a sober analysis of how it was done."

Because Vardon believed that putting is largely a matter of instinct and those faculties supplied by a generous Mother Nature, he declined to offer specific advice on a putting stance and swing. He did say this, however: "In this part of the game, it is quite clear that the right hand has more work to do than the left. It is the right hand that makes the stroke, and therefore I consider that it should be allowed plenty of play, and that the left wrist should be held more loosely than the right." In this, Vardon would find agreement with many of history's great putters, including Willie Park, Walter Travis, Walter Hagen, Horton Smith, Bobby Locke, Billy Casper, and Dave Stockton.

When Tony Lema ran into a bad patch with his putting, he went to Horton Smith for help. "Horton explained that putting was almost entirely a right-handed stroke," Lema wrote in his book, *Golfer's Gold*. "He told me the left hand was there only to help keep the blade on line." Smith suggested Lema try an exercise in which he'd hold the putter only with the right hand and putt from two feet, then four feet, then six feet and finally ten feet. "My stroke and my confidence came back. It was a miracle!" Lema said. Well, for him it was, but he had only been reminded of an old idea from one of golf's finest putters. Walter Hagen, who both Jones and Sarazen cited as the best clutch putter of his time, also wanted the right hand to be in control, and so did Bobby Locke a generation later. Many golfers and modern teachers would disagree, believing that putting like the rest of golf is a two-handed game, or that the left should dominate.

Smith's view is an echo of Willie Park Jr., an early master of putting, who in 1901 wrote: "The right hand should hold more firmly than the left, thus reversing the rule for the grip in other parts of the game. Putting should be almost all done with one hand, because when both hands are used, the one acts against the other; the right hand is the hand that guides the club, and guiding the club is everything in putting, especially in short putts." Putting is too personal a thing to be dogmatic about, but Park's advice and the Horton Smith anecdote are clues that the right vs. left debate has persisted and is likely to continue.

Vardon's admonition about snatching a "sly and careful look" at one's stance is a clue to an attitude toward the other game taken throughout history by a majority of professionals. For the most part, they view putting with suspicion, fear, mistrust, tears, nausea, disdain, or abject disgust. After Vardon's lament, one of the more entertaining insights into putting was Dan Jenkins's piece in *Sports Illustrated*, the magazine he used to work for. The wizards of the day, Dan said, mostly denied they were great putters, and the rest of us, he suggested, might have better chances in the breadlines: "The devoted golfer is an anguished soul who knows a lot about putting, just as an avalanche victim knows a lot about snow. He can't putt and never will. He'd like to bury his head in the dirt and live the rest of his life as a radish." If this sounds all too familiar, you might as well forget all the fancy theories and be guided by the oldest adage of the greens: "The majority of short putts are missed by leaving the ball short of the cup."

Many cite Bobby Locke as the greatest putter. There was an inevitability about his work on the greens that moved Henry Longhurst to write: "One has the impression of Locke that the longer a tournament lasts, the more certain he is to win it. He won tournaments with putting that would be regarded as miraculous for anyone else. For Locke, it was normal. His routine was always the same: the slow weighing of the putting surface, the two little practice swings, the swift, decisive putt with the audible click of club and ball, the pause, the cheers, the solemn touching of the white cap in acknowledgment." Charles Price described how the ball "crept toward the hole and then, just when it was about to stop on the lip, it took one more turn and fell in." Locke said he rarely went for a pin when it was tucked into a tight corner of the green. "What advantage would I gain? If I am putting, I figure to make thirty-foot putts as regularly as I would make the eight-foot putts. One putt is not more difficult than the other. The only difference, old boy, is that one putt is longer than the other." You can imagine how well we'd putt if only we had known this.

Was Bobby Locke (above) the greatest putter? Many think he was, and his method is described nearby. He once went an entire year without three-putting a green.

Locke was so good with the blade that in 1948 he went the whole year without three-putting a green. Did Casper or anyone else match that? Bobby used an old Calamity Jane-style blade putter and used a slightly closed stance. For those who would follow his method, listen to The Mastah: "I address the ball opposite the toe but actually strike the ball with the center of the blade," said Locke. "I do this to avoid cutting the putt. If one addresses the ball with the center of the blade, there is a tendency to swing outside the line on the backswing, resulting in a cutting action. Also, addressing the ball near the toe of the blade makes it easier to take the putter back inside the line and thereby impart topspin at impact. This gives the ball a true end-over-end roll." Did you get all that?

I can't be sure that Locke's stroke was slightly pulled, but it was pretty close. Vardon said the best spin is imparted by the pull, an action he cited in the methods of Willie Park Jr., the marvel of Musselburgh, and Arnaud Massy, the giant Frenchman, two of the deadliest putters he knew. Crenshaw and Player were later marvels who used a pulling motion, and they weren't bad. After a golden era of tap and pop putters led by Casper, Ford, Rosburg, and Thomson, a class of tall, gifted players came along who refined the pendulum stroke to a kind of perfection. Bob Charles and George Archer led this crowd. They kept the hands and wrists very still and stroked with the shoulders. Dave Stockton was deadly using this method. These guys were as good as anyone on the greens, maybe better, so we can't say one method or another is superior. The best of the moderns, Loren Roberts and Brad Faxon, blend some of this with what resembles the putting stroke of Dow Finsterwald, and what a fine one it was, a technique that seemed to rely on feel and solid stroking.

In trying to make sense of such a tender subject, it is at least possible that those who would try to make of putting a purely mechanical business are deluding themselves. Writing in a foreword to the English edition of Bobby Jones's book, *Golf Is My Game*, Bernard Darwin said he very much admired Jones's advice against this sort of thing: "It has so often been tried and always failed in the end, since the dreadful fact remains that the ball 'begs' to be hit." Darwin also admitted that many Englishmen, himself included, "practice our putting in secret a good deal because we are a little ashamed of taking the trouble, and so pretend that we do not." Doug Ford, on the other hand, was never ashamed of practicing at night, slamming putts into the baseboard in his motel room with loud thumps that kept his roommates and everyone else on the same floor wide awake. Putting demons like the sleepless Ford, Paul Runyan, Jerry Barber, and Dave Stockton, none of them born to the golfing purple, you might say, practiced putting for hours on end.

Bobby Jones was a wonder on the greens, using a comfortable stance and wielding the hickory-shafted weapon he named Calamity Jane with a languid, easy stroke.

It is no use prescribing particular stances or strokes, either, because putting is an entirely individual matter. Stockton, who was an absolute wonder on the greens, looked something like a vulture crouching over its prey, legs wide apart like Walter Hagen's and arms akimbo like Leo Diegel's, almost ready to pounce. In fact, Bernard Darwin himself had a vulture's crouch at putting when he was a younger man, a preview if you will of a style of putting adopted half a century later by the tallish Hubert Green, a man who also liked to get down to his business. Nicklaus crouched over his putts, too, with a peculiar off-center stance that gave him a view both of the back of the ball and down the line to the hole. No one holed the pressure putts more consistently than Jack. Isao Aoki putts with the toe of the blade in the air. Brad Faxon stands fairly erect and is perhaps the most orthodox of the modern putting geniuses with the smoothest possible stroke born of a certitude of the ball's fate at the end of it. Bob Jones looked as though he were strolling through the park, and a hint of his mannerism was picked up by Bobby Locke. Tiger Woods is too streaky a putter to hold out as an ideal, but when he is on, his putts cannot be denied the hole. I wonder if it's not a matter of how clearly he sees the line at times, and not so certainly at others.

THE DEVIL WITHIN

Golfers throughout history have wrestled with other mysteries, too: Why is it harder to hit the ball cleanly with a putter than with a driver? Darwin thought it was because we're afraid of it, or afraid of the result. More than with the fuller shots, putting exposes us to the yips, the jerks, the uncertainties, shaky nerves, the fates, outside agencies, and, as Vardon implied, the plain, raw fear of the thing. Apprehension and fear, said Vardon, almost always cause "an involuntary tightening of the grip during the putting swing that causes the body to become rigid." And that's when the body is most likely to move and the putt missed, he concluded. Would a lighter grip promote a smoother stroke? Vardon thought so, but only if you can maintain it throughout the stroke. Paul Runyan thought it better to use a firm grip from beginning to end, believing it wouldn't tighten suddenly. But there's no guarantee that it wouldn't.

Sam McKinlay, the crack golf writer for the *Glasgow Herald*, was a fine player as well who was regularly chosen to play for the Scottish team in matches against England. He was a member of the British Walker Cup team in 1934, and in 1947 he reached the semifinals of the British Amateur Championship. McKinlay described running into a bad patch with his putting, which he cured for a while by recalling a favorite passage from a piano concerto. "Something of the rhythm crept into my stroke and what had been for all too long a scuffling stab became smooth and fluid. So effective was it that I had only to recapture the music and long putts went stone dead and the little ones went in with a Casper plop. It was wonderful while it lasted, but alas, although the melody lingers on, the song has ended."

With obviously more imagination than skill, we are adept at devising dozens of ways to trick the devils within us. There is the upright style and the crouched one; the technique of elbows out like Leo Diegel and Phil Rodgers, or elbows in like Arnold Palmer and Bob Rosburg, both disciples of George Low. Some like Hubert Green prefer to attack with the legs wide apart, while angels like Bobby Jones preferred the legs together. Some can only take their medicine up close by gripping down the shaft as

Joe Turnesa did, while others prefer to take it at a distance by holding the wand at the top as Lloyd Mangrum and Jerry Barber did. Gary McCord has tried his best yet hadn't earned a single victory in more than twenty years on both the regular and senior tours in spite of a commendable long game. Look no further than his hesitant acquaintance with the putting arts. In recent times, McCord tried seven different putting grips and styles during a Senior Open in Chicago while playing partners Raymond Floyd and Hale Irwin were unable to conceal their laughter. These two putting wizards were laughing not at McCord, poor fellow, but because they understood the peculiar and, for some, perverse demands of that other game.

In the 1960s, several fine ball strikers unable to fathom the mysteries of putting stumbled upon the croquet style, which saved

With age, players like Sam Snead turned to the croquet stance to steady their stroke, and when that was banned by the USGA because it was "unsightly," moved over to the sidesaddle version seen above.

their careers, at least for a while. Among the earliest of these, I believe, was Ernie Vossler who was named the tour's Rookie of the Year in 1967, although the magic didn't last. Several fellows improved on Vossler's technique, including at least one immortal, Sam Snead, and one U. S. Open winner, Orville Moody, who later was one of the first to adapt to the super-long putter. When Snead jumped on the bandwagon, the USGA was more or less appalled and banned the croquet style. Sam, never a man to fight city hall, simply adapted his stance to a sidesaddle version that conformed well enough to the rules. Moody, a superb ball-striker with wood and iron, was baffled by putting. He tried every nostrum, including— unsuccessfully—putting with the left hand below the right; this style is gaining favor today, but it did little for him. Others tried putting while looking at the hole, or while closing their eyes, by resorting to

Chris DiMarco uses The Claw and a super-long putter, one of many methods, including the "Belly" style, devised to steady an uncertain putting stroke. Purists among both players and officials believe these should be banned.

incantations, or prayers. George Low spun tales of pros in the 1930s who would spit on their golf ball when they had a swift downhiller, a bit of chicanery that kept their putts from rolling too far. But, said Low, Ky Laffoon and others who chewed tobacco couldn't apply the juice without being detected by tour officials.

Those fellows were colorful but not as resourceful as the moderns have turned out to be. The present crowd has devised any number of tricks and dodges to conquer the yips, notably The Claw and variations like The Saw, adapted successfully by Mark O'Meara. Apparently The Claw was started by Skip Kendall, who passed it on to Mark Calcavecchia, Chris DiMarco, Kevin Sutherland, and others. This gave way to the Belly Job, a method used rather successfully by Phil Rodgers back in the 1970s, and tried by Paul Runyan even earlier, and in recent times embraced by Vijay Singh, Scott McCarron, Paul Azinger, and Colin Montgomerie. This style appalls purists; Ernie Els would like to ban it, and even some of the converts feel sheepish using it. Darren Clarke, who tried the method briefly, admitted: "Even though I'm using the belly putter, it definitely shouldn't be allowed." These players don't look very comfortable doing it, and I suppose they're not, but they manage the deed nevertheless. Putting can be such a humiliating business, as Hogan and others came to know and eventually resist, but they must do it.

In Europe, superb ball strikers like Bernhard Langer and Sam Torrance, whose dad, Bob Torrance, had a lifelong reputation as a solid, sensible golf teacher, took up the cudgel when their putting strokes deserted them. They did well. Langer might be a special case because he was afflicted by the yips in three different decades, and each time he brought the creature to heel. This is an

Bernhard Langer has overcome the yips several times using desperate measures like the one above in which he pins the putter handle against his left forearm with a clutching grab of the right hand, an old defense dating back more than a hundred years.

extraordinary achievement all by itself and yet another measure of the German's dogged determination. When we look back, however, we see that Langer's frightened, awkward clutches, in which he jammed the putter handle into his left arm while holding on for dear life with the right hand was an old defense. In an early story, Bernard Darwin described a St. Andrews golfer of the 1890s who attempted to master the yips by shoving the putter shaft "inside the sleeve of his coat in order to get a rigid, immobile wrist," and it wouldn't surprise me to learn that this idea had been tried even earlier. As you have noticed, not much in golf is really new.

Nearly everyone from Vardon to Jones, from Finsterwald to Faxon seems to agree on one thing, however: no matter what method you use, learn to hit your putts solidly. That's easy enough to say, but not everyone would know how to go about finding a solid stroke. Bob Rosburg was one of the best putters of the twentieth century. He once wrote a textbook on the subject that offered a fairly simple, practical way to learn what a solid putting stroke feels like. "Find a straight, uphill, three-to-four-footer on your practice putting clock. This putt will go in if the ball is given a firm, straight tap. If the stroke is uncertain or wobbly, the ball will almost surely stop short or go off-line. When you start knocking in these easy four-footers with regularity, you're on the way to building a solid putting stroke." Bob always advocated a short, firm, accelerating rap, and practiced what he preached.

Experts agree we should all learn to hit putts solidly. Bob Rosburg, a putting demon, never cared much for practice but wrote a book on putting in which he explained a simple way to learn what a solid putting stroke feels like.

Peter Allis, the glib golf analyst, was one of England's better players for years and became familiar to Americans as a member of eight British Ryder Cup teams before he moved to the television booth. Allis has said he never saw a great putter who did not look comfortable at his work, but I can't say that Palmer ever gave the impression of comfort or ease over his putts—more

The great putters settle on a method and practice until it becomes part of them. Brad Faxon, one of the best of the moderns, says the secret of his success on the greens is he doesn't worry whether the ball goes in the hole or not.

like a crouched panther eyeing its prey. So it doesn't matter how you look to others or what method you use, only the results. Look at Billy Mayfair, who owns the most outrageous putting stroke of modern times, an action fairly described as two loops and a cut. Mayfair cold slices his putts, every one, and yet most of them find the bottom of the cup. What seems to matter in putting is that the good putters settle on their own method and practice it long hours every day until it becomes part of them.

"The best putters under pressure," according to Cary Middlecoff who was himself one of the best, are those "who had to work the hardest to become great putters—guys like Ben Hogan, Jack Nicklaus, Jerry Barber, and Paul Runyan. I did, too." Not that he wore himself out; practice was not Middlecoff's favorite way to pass the time. "I used to admire Hogan and his determination," said Cary. "He would beat balls for two or three hours, maybe all day, and then go putt for hours. My limit was forty-five minutes; after that, I'd lose my concentration. Everyone's different. Sam Snead used to enjoy hitting those one-irons and two-irons in practice, shot after perfect shot. There is a thrill in hitting shots on the practice range, just watching them. It's just not the same thrill when you practice putting, no matter how many balls you hole."

Imagine a fellow with Middlecoff's reputation on the greens spending just forty minutes practicing his putting. What an extraordinary man! Certainly not one to emulate if we hope to improve our scores. Even Willie Park Jr., the nineteenth-century wizard, was said to have practiced putting at least four hours a day, Paul Runyan the same, and Jose Maria Olazabal, Brad Faxon, and other present-day wonders, can be placed on Doc Middlecoff's own list of those who have practiced the other game until they were masters. If you or I had devoted that same amount of time to practicing putting, we, too, would be sick of it. Faxon, by the way, has said that the secret to his wondrous putting is that he doesn't worry about whether it goes in or not. With his stroke, why would he?

Tommy Bolt's plaintive rant quoted at the top of this chapter may stand as the truest thing ever uttered about putting, speaking as it does for many of his fellow pros and millions of us.

Ben Crenshaw has been a super putter for fifty years. It started when he was two, and hasn't changed. One story is that he doesn't have to practice all that much because it comes so naturally to him, but that would hardly be fair.

"Putting is the department of the game with which each man must wrestle by himself in silence and sorrow," wrote Bernard Darwin. That sounds about right, although there are plenty of gurus around like Dave Pelz and Stan Utley who are willing to set us on the right path. Someone told me the other day that Pelz was the highest paid golf instructor in the United States, maybe in the world. I don't know if that's true or not, but if it is, I imagine it's a measure of how important "the other game" really is.

Or is Hogan's to be the last, blunt word on the subject: "If you want to improve your putting, hit it closer to the hole," Ben said. Maybe it was watching all those brilliant iron shots by his Texas neighbor Byron Nelson. "Byron knocked it so close, Ray Charles coulda made the putts," chuckled Lee Trevino. He might also have mentioned Tom Kite who, according to an exhaustive study by Dave Pelz, put his short approaches closer to the flagstick than anyone on the tour. According to that same study, Trevino himself was the greatest shot-making artist, tee to green, of his generation. He gave much of the credit to "Helen," an old Wilson Helen Hicks model wedge with a dimpled face and a limber shaft he found in a barrel of used clubs and bought for two bucks. "Helen won a bunch of majors and I can't tell you how much loose change," Lee said. Kite was one of the first to carry three wedges in his bag; for all we know he might have carried more if the fourteen-club limit were lifted. Geniuses, both, whose fabulous gifts in the short game certainly didn't hurt their work on the greens. A natural successor is Mike Weir, the cool Canadian left-hander, whose victories in the 2003 Masters and other big tournaments have come to him largely owing to a magical wedge game combined with a steely putting stroke. Weir is also a straight driver; John Daly is not.

The massive Daly won the Buick Invitational at San Diego early in 2004, his first victory after nine years in the wilderness, by reining in his great power, staying very patient, and relying on a superb, under-appreciated short game. Daly is deadly around the greens from grass or sand, and his long, unhurried putting stroke, with its fine judgment of distance, bears an uncanny resemblance to Bobby Jones's—although the two were as different as men could be in size, temperament, and so many other ways. On the final hole at Torrey Pines, Daly pitched his ball a hundred feet from the sand stone dead, a winning stroke. He said afterward:

"You win tournaments with your short game. I won both the PGA Championship and the British Open with my short game, and this one, too."

Any attempt to explain putting logically or to put a face on it is doomed. In the end, it is given to some, not to others, and sometimes only loaned for a while. You can pick anyone you like as a model, and hope for the best—Casper's tap, Nicklaus's piston-stroke, Charles's shoulder-stroke, Crenshaw's languid pull, or Locke's brush-and-jab. There was and still is more than a touch of Locke in Gary Player's putting stroke. Closed stance, shortish jab with a pulling action, a brisk scrape of blade upon turf, and off the ball rolls, claiming the hole as its own. Player did this for forty years on seven continents, and he's still doing it in his late sixties.

What can we make of this? The physical fitness? More like the mental fitness; perhaps the two are linked, but if Gary Player has shown us anything it is surely how the mental controls the physical. It is probably true, as many books and articles on the subject claim, that Nicklaus has holed more crucial putts than anyone in history (although greybeards may remember Jones), but I wonder if anyone has actually measured Gary's record in this category against Jack's. You wouldn't go far wrong in wanting to copy Player's method, and his will to hole out.

CHAPTER
EIGHT

GOLF FROM THE NECK UP

"Golf is the one game I know that becomes more and more difficult the longer one plays it." —Bobby Jones

After playing golf for forty years, only two things ever bothered me about the game: Distance and Direction. Well, trajectory, too, if you must be picky. Years ago, the golf magazine I worked for held seminars once or twice a year in which the editors met with an expert panel of advisors (read professional stars) who were paid to appear on our masthead. Our owners believed, with unerring judgment, that we needed the stature. At these seminars, we would spend a day or two discussing the golf swing and the issues of the day with a view to developing story ideas for the coming season. In one of the sessions, the gurus of golf had argued for hours over intricate details of the golf swing and a couple of hot new teaching theories that had the panelists at each other's throats.

Through all of this, Byron Nelson had held himself pretty much above the fray, but finally our editor, Dick Aultman, a lovely man of gentle disposition who was invariably entranced with fine points of golf instruction, turned to Lord Byron and asked for an opinion. The discussion had covered the most bewildering array of detail and swing minutiae, so when Nelson said, with just the hint of a smile: "Well, it seems to me there are only two problems in golf—distance and direction," I knew he had us, and, of course, I couldn't help but love a man who had correctly diagnosed my own two problems in golf.

It is when we parse the sentence too finely that it dissolves and leaves us without understanding or context. The same with the golf swing. I think Byron was as confused as the rest of us about where this discussion was leading, but I also believe he was trying to gently prod the discussion back to the center and common sense. Some years later, the panel found itself in a similar hot debate on a fine point of the swing, and this time it was Sam

The roots of wisdom lie in simplicity, at least in golf they do, as Byron Nelson reminded us during a prolonged discussion of the fine details of golf instruction. There are only two problems in golf, said Byron with a smile.

Snead who ended things with the simplest of answers. In the years I spent listening to great players, my impression has been that they almost always home in on the simple answer. Some of our experts, like Paul Runyan and Cary Middlecoff, tended to be more technical because their minds needed to be satisfied on that level before they could accept and explain a physical move or principle. Some of us are like that, too, and any golf teacher worth his or her hourly rate knows this and is prepared to offer a technical explanation when the occasion arises and the pupil needs it.

On the other side of the street are the simplifiers. John Jacobs said, "The only object of the golf swing is to present the club correctly to the ball," By that he meant presenting it with "a square face, along the correct swing path, at the proper angle of attack, and at a speed required for the shot." The ball doesn't care how this is done; that's the good news. The bad news is that we are obliged to deal with all those variables to make the ball go where we want it to go. Happily, there are a thousand or perhaps ten thousand different ways we can swing to accomplish the desired goal. Yet that is often the source of our trouble. "One reason I have always thought that golf can be such a difficult game is simply that there are so many ways of playing it correctly," Jacobs said in an interview at his induction into the World Golf Hall of Fame, in 2001. "One secret for any golfer striving to improve is to decide which is his or her correct way."

Those very differences are what make teaching the game difficult, too. What Snead and Nicklaus felt is not the same as what you and I feel, at least I don't think it is. Nor can you and I experience what Armour and Toski felt when they were playing in the heat of top professional competition. The words that Hogan and his collaborator Herb Wind chose to express Ben's ideas on the "basics" are different from those of his own contemporaries like George Fazio and Dutch Harrison, both of whom had exquisitely developed insights into the mechanics of the golf swing. The swings of each man were as leisurely as a cat licking its fur and, like Hogan, there wasn't a shot they couldn't hit. Hogan eventually arrived at a purer swing, perhaps, although more violent than theirs. Some of the

John Jacobs (coaching a pupil above) has said the reason golf is so difficult is simply that there are so many ways of playing it correctly, which is one source of our trouble because we must then decide which way is correct for us.

things in Hogan's book, *Five Lessons*, were then and are even now still debated. "Ben tried very hard in that book to make his ideas clear, and it must have discouraged him to find himself not much better understood," observed Cary Middlecoff, who went on to acknowledge how difficult it is for a teacher to get his points across in a book or magazine.

Maybe what we duffers really need is a simpler model, not dumber but simpler concepts and words. More like Tommy Armour or

John Jacobs or Arnold Palmer. Arnold Palmer? I remember those four Masters victories and those exciting charges of his, but I don't recall seeing his name among all those lists of the top hundred golf teachers in America. No, but the lessons Arnold learned from his father, Deacon Palmer, were passed along by the son to friends and have been chronicled in several books. Not surprisingly, these were given serious attention by Cary Middlecoff, who was a keen student of the golf swing and very much in his element when he was analyzing golf techniques and theories. Middlecoff thought it revealing that in *My Game and Yours*, one of Arnold's popular books on how to play golf, he devoted twice as many pages to the mental as he did to the mechanical aspects of golf, and cited Deacon Palmer's dictum: "Ninety percent of golf is played from the shoulders up."

Cary Middlecoff (left) and Ben Hogan (right) were friends and frequent playing companions, men with inquisitive, analytic minds who shared a fascination with the golf swing.

Palmer's views about the game are fascinating, not only because of his impact on golf and on several generations of golfers, but for the practical and sound advice he offers. "The swing is the easiest part of golf. Once you've got the right grip and if you hold your head steady, it is almost impossible to swing badly," Palmer said. The rest is mental and emotional, and few men have ridden these two horses longer than Palmer.

BACKSWINGS

Listen to the gurus talk and you will hear whispers of "the takeaway" and "modern techniques of the backswing," or some such. Swinging the club back beyond parallel, according to some modern theory, is not necessary for length and can actually be harmful to accuracy. Just look at Tiger Woods's position at the top of the swing, which often fails to reach parallel, and watch his tee shots soar to distances barely contemplated B. C. (Before Callaway). Well, explain that to Ben Hogan and Don January and John Daly, all of whom swung back so far past parallel that the club pointed to the ground at the "top" of the backswing. Even when he modified and shortened his swing, Hogan still swung the driver back past parallel. Hogan and Daly have been two of the longest hitters in the history of golf, and I don't recall anyone suggesting that Hogan was not accurate. January was a top player for years. While Daly has experienced an occasional lapse of direction in his adventurous career, I don't suppose that he is that much less accurate than many of the men who compete on the pro tours. So this business of the club's position at the top of the backswing can be seen largely as a matter of individual build, flexibility, and, probably more to the point, an adaption to the habits of early youth.

The only purpose of the backswing, John Jacobs reminded us, is to place the club in a position to deliver a correct blow to the ball, and Byron Nelson agreed. From benches opposite, Sam Snead and Bob Jones expressed the view that the backswing was integral to the overall rhythm of the swing. Others claim that we should start the backswing like a windup toy—lift the club straight in front of the body,

John Daly swings back so far his club almost points to the ground, a flaw according to some experts, but this swing characteristic may be less a flaw than his own flexibility and an adaption to the habits of early youth.

cock the wrists, turn the upper body slowly into position and check it all out before delivering a downswing at full speed. Good luck, Clyde! This might work if humans were wired like Iron Byron, that magnificent , hypnotic ball-striking machine built by True Temper—so named by USGA golf editor Bob Sommers because it was modeled on Byron Nelson's swing—but we're not.

When we look at it objectively, the movements of a golf swing are as intricate as a fine watch and need to be as finely, though not so mechanically, tuned. The notions that we can control the action by conscious thought, or that we can somehow correct it during the downswing, are not very realistic, either. As his one-time teacher, Butch Harmon, has said, "Even the great Tiger Woods can't do that all the time." Commenting on some of Tiger's errant swings during the 2001 major championships, Harmon pointed to his being only slightly out of position at the top of the swing. "When you don't get in the right position at the top of the swing, maybe getting the hands too far behind, you try to correct that with speed by trying to catch up with your hands. In this, Tiger is no different from anyone else. Once Tiger got in the right position and everything matched up, he felt comfortable and shot beautiful rounds of golf. Golf is a fickle game; even the best players in the world struggle." In such a finely tuned swing as Tiger's and swinging with his enormous speed, the margin for error is tiny. For the rest of us who swing with much less speed, there is more room for error, perhaps, but the principle is the same. In Harmon's view, the position of the club and clubface at the top of the backswing is something worth paying attention to.

Jack Nicklaus also liked the notion that the backswing is used to "set the club in proper position for starting the forward swing," but he has said too that the secret purpose of the backswing is to "build up energy" so it isn't wasted. Nicklaus said as well that a slow, wide backswing with a full turn of the body is more likely to build energy. Well, okay, but what if my natural swing speed is more like Tom Watson's or Jesper Parnevik's or Nick Price's? Or Ben Hogan's, for that matter. Those guys all had fast swings. Admittedly, mine and yours are probably not as technically sound, but can we weekend golfers ignore our natural tempo? Should we?

Even the best players struggle with their swings, as Tiger Woods's former teacher, Butch Harmon (left), explains nearby. Tiger's margin of error is much smaller than yours or mine, but the principles are the same.

"Nature, Mr. Allnut, is what we are put into this world to rise above," said the prissy missionary played by Katharine Hepburn to a rough-hewn Humphrey Bogart in *The African Queen*. The evangelical zeal Miss Hepburn voices in the film shares similar roots with certain methods of golf instruction. At bottom, preachers of any stripe will assert eternal truths easily found under the banner of their doctrine. Religion and golf are somewhat alike in this. Human behavior is not to be trusted, they suspect, which means that certain correctives must (there's that lovely word again) be applied, and the learned gentlemen will have you understand that they know best what these correctives shall be.

In most things we do, golf included, we are better off settling for things that work. As Mr. Allnutt had discovered, the use of his native faculties always seemed to come in handy when he needed them most. It was a truth he had learned and verified by practical application, by teaching himself to cope with physics and nature as he found them, rather than being tempted by rarified concepts of an appealing but unserviceable moral doctrine. If golf is anything in the physical sense, it is brutally practical. Cause and effect rules on every shot. We cannot escape it, which is why fellows like Ben Hogan and George Schoux and Vijay Singh practiced so many hours: each man hoped to interject his own will between the two.

What do we mean by "natural?" We have all experienced the discomfort of training our natural impulses to adapt to a sound method of doing something. In golf, this usually means learning a new move and, with help and demonstration by a golf professional, we can see why it's useful. We may also be lucky enough to see the difference between our "natural" impulse and what can be accomplished more efficiently and fluently by following the laws of nature. This goes back to the ball flight laws discussed in Chapter Three, and how we arrange ourselves and our golf swings to obey them. This doesn't mean forcing our bodies into unnatural moves. Nature always follows lines of least resistance; it is direct and opportunistic. We see this in the behavior of water and lightning, both of which yield to gravity and other natural opportunities.

Those who wear eyeglasses know something of this phenomenon. When the doctor changes a patient's prescription, there is usually a period of adjustment before the eyes and brain accommodate to the new eyeglasses. Often this is accompanied by discomfort, even pain as the muscles of the eyes strain to fit the new optics. The eyes make this adjustment *automatically* without any conscious effort by the patient other than the imposition of new lenses. By the same process, donning someone else's eyeglasses whose prescription is different from one's own will bring a violent reaction as the eye muscles strain to adjust to the wrong prescription. Ultimately, they will rebel. They do this without our bidding. I imagine that the same sort of process is at work in our golf swings.

Such autonomic, some might say instinctive, reactions are what I mean by the term *natural*. Fighting one's natural disposition may actually induce the very swing faults we are trying so earnestly to prevent. We can't avoid a certain amount of discomfort in golf, especially at the beginning, but it is less painful, and probably more effective to keep things simple. Peter Thomson is an example of someone who became a great player by his wits and his natural instincts. Bred on Mackenzie courses in Australia, his swing was based on a simple model—swing back and through. Although he won five British Opens and many other titles around the world and was sorely tempted by publishers, Thomson never wrote an instruction book because, he said, there was not much more than that to say about the golf swing. He must have gone through bad patches now and again but Peter didn't allow complicated thoughts to interfere with his intentions. Swing back and through, hit the ball forward, and pop it into the hole when you get to the putting surface.

Simplicity is greatly admired by the gods. Those who study the golf swing perhaps more than is good for them will know that Bobby Jones was a great admirer of Joyce Wethered's swing; he called it the model for aspiring golfers of either gender. Jones pointed to both the simplicity and the grace of Miss Wethered's golf swing, features he noted were matched in the swing of Horton Smith. Jones was particularly taken with Smith's backswing, which he called the simplest in the world. In these ideal swings, said Jones, "the matter of hitting of a ball has been reduced to two

Two of the finest swings, according to Bobby Jones, belonged to English-woman Joyce Wethered (left), the consummate amateur, and Horton Smith (right), the American professional. Both swings were marked by simplicity and grace.

motions, taking the club back with one, and bringing it down with the other." Simple and direct, just as practical souls like Thomson would have it.

PLAYING GOLF

It is in the playing of the game, though, that we need the mind. Start with Vardon, Jones, Hogan, and Nicklaus. Learn what they learned. Know what they knew. Does anyone remember what a deliberate and conservative player Nicklaus was? You might even say timid until you watched him putt; nothing timid there. Jack was known in his day as the most deliberate player in the game, easily a match for his fidgety Florida neighbor Cary Middlecoff. Nicklaus knew the game was getting the ball in the hole, but of course, many others knew this. What set him apart was how willingly he took the safe or most sensible route home—to lay up when he should, to aim away from danger, and, yes, to crash a long one into the far rough when the percentage was with him and he knew he'd have only a flick into the green. That was the majesty of his game.

To gamble was not Jack's way. It violated his sense of order, and if he wanted to do anything in life it was to control things. How does one control a game like golf? By controlling one's self, we learn, and Nicklaus may have done this better than any other player since Jones. More than intellect was at work here. Jones was more cerebral, maybe Hogan, too, than Nicklaus, but it seems to me that lately only Tiger Woods has combined the Nicklaus qualities of mind and will, although Jack was more patient than Woods even as a younger man. Nicklaus would take chances when the odds were with him, but rarely when they were not, in response to the competitive situation.

What a terrible thing it must be to come upon a shot fraught with risk but well within your grasp and yet know that it must be resisted, and then actually to resist it! That inner conflict is a constant test of competitive golf and a defining one at its highest levels, where the talent is usually there to pull off almost any shot, from almost any lie. That is the immeasurable but critical difference of mind between Nicklaus and Weiskopf, between Annika and her pursuers. This is something we miserable weekenders, too, seem only dimly to grasp or appreciate. The longer we play the game the more opportunities we have to learn this, but, as Jones has warned us, the tougher it gets.

Jack Nicklaus was a powerful golfer who could hit any golf shot, but understood the game so well that he could almost always resist the low percentage play. That inner conflict is a defining test of competitive golf at the highest levels.

THE MAGNIFICENT PARADOX

When Jones, with credit to his sportswriter friend O. B. Keeler, made that wry observation about the most important distance in golf being the five or six inches between our ears, he was reminding us of the magnificent paradox of the game in which mental discipline and emotional control, or their lack, are the ultimate

196

masters of technique. Golf seems at first to be grounded in those practical, simple matters of physical movement and method that can so aggravate us at times, and which also are the sources of so much of our pleasure. But soon we learn that mastering a golf swing does not always lead to mastery of the game. Many experience the momentary glory of flush contact and the delight of watching a ball soar into the distance, or the satisfaction of a long putt holed over a rolling green. These are set against the moments of failure, the gouged chip, the topped fairway wood, the trembling two-footer missed at the end.

We face more than one paradox in golf, of course. There is the need for both caution and courage, and the tug between our emotions and our muscles and their unstable fuel supply of adrenaline. The game invites us to bash and smash, then snatches away our satisfaction by causing the ball to sail into the woods or fall pathetically short into water. For the ball to go up, we hit down. To go left, we aim right; to go right, we aim left; to hit far, we swing easy. The golf swing is a tangle of contradictions and enigmas, even before we take the bloody thing to the golf course.

The moment we have learned how to hit shots with reasonable consistency, our confidence swells and we are off to the fairways to tackle the beast. It is then we get a taste of another paradox, expressed by Jacobs and many others, that hitting golf shots is a fairly simple business while playing the game is anything but. Faced with actual dimensions into which we must fit our shots and hazards that wish to claim them, our muscles tighten and our swings are no longer as free. Shots fly in every direction, and we are soon playing too many of them from deep woods or thick grass, and that's the end of confidence. Back we march to the practice range and our favorite guru to seek solace and salvation.

Sometimes the prescribed therapy is a playing lesson so that the golf pro can observe us under pressure and sprinkle soothing phrases over our anxieties.

TOSKI'S PLAYING LESSONS

In the case of very good players, playing lessons are rarely useful because the problem can usually be traced to a fundamental cause like ball position, alignment, or the like. Even with beginners and medium level players, the lasting efficacy of playing lessons is doubtful. Although not every method is catalogued, I have seen only one truly effective approach to playing lessons, the one used by Bob Toski. Here again, we have a teacher who played at the very highest levels and knows the game intimately at its best and at its worst. He met the temptations of greed and arrogance and all the others, and, owing to the talent he and such fellows have, probably bested them as often as he failed. This is the fellow (and others like him) I want to teach me how to play the game.

Toski's method goes like this: Tee it up and let 'er fly. If the ball goes in the fairway, fine; hit the second and succeeding shots until you reach the green. If a shot falls into the rough or a bunker, or the water, or indeed any place off the fairway, collect the ball, march back ten to fifteen yards and place it in the fairway without penalty and continue your play until you reach the green. Repeat this procedure every time the ball finishes off the fairway or the green. Keep track of your score, and compare it with your normal scores. Toski has kept pretty good statistics on this and reckons most players save as many as a dozen strokes or more using this method. A stroke in the fairway is worth two in the bush, you might say.

"Golf is a game of distance and direction, and direction comes first," Toski says. He also points out that golfers, especially youngsters, who swing violently and out of control are only preparing themselves for disaster. "Most golfers prepare themselves for failure, while good players prepare themselves for success," he adds. Toski's playing lesson teaches clearly that in playing the game, you will almost always score better by keeping the ball on the short grass. Obviously,

Bob Toski devised a practical way to test a golfer's judgment and ability to score. It teaches the value of keeping the ball on the fairway and away from rough and hazards, and saves many strokes.

you can do it more often by not trying to hit the ball quite so hard. If you want to lower your handicap, then, this is a most practical way to learn. Another involves the short game, which is another matter entirely and is dealt with in Toski's elegantly simple method of learning to play from the hole out, which is described in Chapter Two.

FACES

Once upon a time I found myself engaged in a warm dispute with a golf professional, no less, about the position of the clubface in the backswing. My understanding was that, assuming the golfer has placed his or her hands in a more or less conventional grip on the handle, when the face of the club points to the sky at the top of the backswing, it is "shut," while this fellow asserted the opposite. "It is open!" he declared. We went on for about ten minutes arguing the opposing points of view, but I soon realized that this fellow's opinion was embedded in granite and that no authority on earth would dislodge it. I crept away on tiptoe, with a silent wish that I might never be paired with him, either in conversation or in friendly competition.

This sort of misunderstanding is quite common among golfers, even good ones, and, as we've just seen, professionals. The only reason to bother about "open" and "shut" faces is to gain a better understanding about the shape of our shots. Most of the wise men over the past two hundred years agree with the general notion that the position of the clubface at impact determines the direction a golf ball will curve in flight, if at all. When the clubhead is angled at impact so that the toe of the club is ahead of the heel, the face is closed, or shut. When the clubhead is angled at impact so that the toe of the club is behind the heel, the face is open. A neutral face in which the toe and heel are even at impact is said to be "square" to the swing path and will theoretically produce a shot that curves very little in flight. Much as I despise diagrams with arrows and such, the adjoining sketch will demonstrate, I hope clearly, what is meant by this.

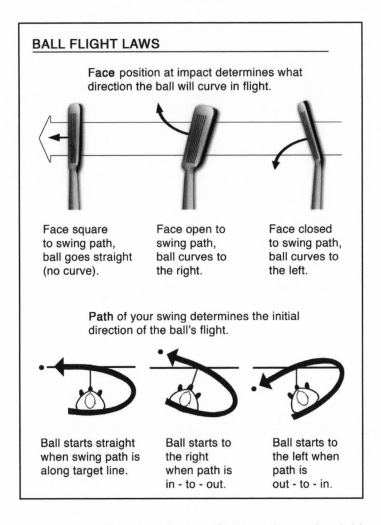

BALL FLIGHT LAWS

Face position at impact determines what direction the ball will curve in flight.

Face square to swing path, ball goes straight (no curve).

Face open to swing path, ball curves to the right.

Face closed to swing path, ball curves to the left.

Path of your swing determines the initial direction of the ball's flight.

Ball starts straight when swing path is along target line.

Ball starts to the right when path is in - to - out.

Ball starts to the left when path is out - to - in.

Common sense will explain the rest. Since we know the clubhead is traveling at speed, the initial direction the ball goes is more or less forward—physics dictates that its initial direction will be exactly opposite to the force of the impact, and will go exactly along its line. When the face is angled either open or shut, the ball will spin in the direction the face is "looking." This is more detailed than anything I had wished to explain in this otherwise untechnical book, but since the point under discussion is not instruction but physics, I hope it's forgivable to include. It's also very much a part of those ball flight laws discussed in Chapter Three.

Here's something you can tuck away for future reference. When you are reading an instruction article in a golf magazine or watching a pointer on television, any swing photographs or video sequence swings that do not show the clubface all the way through are more or less worthless in diagnosing the point and in showing what is truly happening. The reason goes back to those laws of ball flight—if the clubface is either open or closed to the path of the swing, the ball will curve in flight (the only exception is in playing out of sand when the clubface contacts the sand, not the ball). It is that curving in flight that gives us fits when the swerve is unintentional; more importantly, it affects how we will swing on the next shot, whether we like it or not.

THE LINK WITH PATH

Sensible readers are warned to skip the next two paragraphs. An argument developed during the 1960s and 1970s over which was the more basic influence on the shape of a golf shot, the clubface at impact or the path of the swing? Those who argued "face "had history on their side. When a kid picks up a golf club for the first time he has no idea where the face is aiming when the club contacts the ball; he concentrates only on hitting the ball. The face is left to its own devices. If the shot curves left, he will react with some kind of correction, conscious or not, on the next shot. The same if the shot curves right. This, say the advocates of "face first," is the primary influence on a golfer's swing, and is a governing influence on all future swings. Those who argue for "path" follow a more subtle reasoning. Using the same example of the beginner, if the path of the swing is out-to-in, this will cause an involuntary opening of the face as the club nears impact. This happens because the mind's eye wants the ball to go toward the target, no matter what the golfer has done. As a result, the ball will curve from left to right because of the spin caused by the open face. If the path is in-to-out, the face of the club does just the opposite, it closes involuntarily and for the same reasons. So, the "path-minders" would claim that the face is always changing, however slightly, in response to the path of the swing.

Who is right? Who knows? John Jacobs had analyzed this more carefully, I think, than any golf teacher until that time. John was a "face" man for most of his career, believing that golfers react instantly to slices and hooks and their bodies respond accordingly. Sometime in the late 1970s he began to have second thoughts, and as far as I know, he never quite resolved this question. I haven't noticed any definitive studies on the subject since then, but you and I needn't worry. The answer is more important to those whose job it is to root out the causes of our swing faults. You and I have only to follow the evidence of our eyes—watch the flight of the ball—and use a bit of common sense.

BACK TO THE HEAD GAMES

To be certain in the mind of these simple, basic notions about the golf swing is to gain a sense of confidence in one's method and eventually it gives us a measure of tranquility about our game. This is not all, but it's a fine start. Bobby Jones, who had a right to have as much confidence in his own game as anyone, wrote about the real demons he faced in competitive golf. The fear that gripped him most was a kind of uncertainty about finishing off an opponent or a tournament. "Whatever lack others many have seen in me, the one I felt most was the absolute inability to continue smoothly and with authority to wrap up a championship after I had won command of it," said Jones. "This failing cost me winning more than one championship." In analyzing why, Jones said: "I became fearful of making myself look ridiculous by kicking the thing away. I think I began to be conscious of my swing and trying to be too certain of avoiding a disastrous mistake." These same alarm bells have rung for players in every era. "The person I fear most in the last two rounds is myself," said Tom Watson, in a moment of candor during his peak. Bob Jones said it wasn't in playing safe that he went wrong, but in failing "to play definitely for the safe objective." In other words, choose a safe route and play for it decisively. Does that sound like Nicklaus? Ever slowly do we learn.

The fear that gripped Bobby Jones in the heat of competition wasn't much different from any other golfer's; he was afraid of looking ridiculous in front of friends and the multitudes.

Using our heads takes many forms. Years ago, I was

paired in a pro-am with Mickey Rooney, a fine actor whose obsession with golf and with a celebrity guru named Count Yogi was too apparent. Yogi had imparted to Rooney the secret of golf, which was to pose on the follow-through with perfect form. Do this and all ills will be cured, said the energetic Rooney, who was kind enough to remind us of it on nearly every hole. While there is probably some benefit in this for golfers whose swings are otherwise restricted, the truth is that the follow-through is a result, not a cause of a sound swing. To work back from the end of things, then, is probably most effective as a diagnostic tool. The clearest proof of this is the "punch shot," that indispensable tool of champion golfers from Harry Vardon to Tiger Woods. Vardon called it a "push shot." Ben Hogan called it his money shot. When the young Gardner Dickinson came to work for Hogan at Tamarisk in Palm Springs, California, Hogan took him to the range and asked if Gardner had a safety shot, one that he could depend upon when the heat was on, and asked him to demonstrate. After Dickinson hit a crisp punch with a middle-iron, Hogan growled: "Damn right!"

The punch shot is struck with a sharp, descending stroke marked by a shortish follow-through and a low ball flight. The stroke is usually cut off rather abruptly at about waist to shoulder height after contact. The most majestic example of the art I can recall is that of Roberto DeVicenzo, a powerful man who was among the world's longest hitters. Roberto's punched irons tore through the winds of Hoylake helping the Argentinian win the 1967 British Open and over two hundred other tournaments. There was an unhurried grace about those shots, which sounded like mortars whistling past your ear. Tiger Woods plays this stroke better than any of the contemporary stars; I believe he calls it a "stinger."

Woods uses it just like Vardon and Hogan and DeVicenzo—whenever he needs to keep the ball in the fairway or when he absolutely must find a green. I can't think of a first-class player of the last fifty years who doesn't.

So to say that there must be no check to the swing, that the arms and club must sail freely around the body and finish alongside the player's cap is not all that can be said about the swing and is not, after all, a universal objective. To have the punch shot in one's arsenal is a useful ambition for any golfer, and knowing when to use it (more often than you might imagine) is part of the mental game. However, be warned that the punch is an advanced technique, and for many golfers it is probably best left to a future day.

Roberto DeVicenzo holds his follow-through after hitting a powerful punch shot during his winning effort in the 1967 Open Championship at Hoylake, England where he finished two strokes ahead of Nicklaus.

THE 'X' FACTOR

Human kind contains within its genes an almost universal desire for improvement—better food, better shelter, better mates, better climate, and so on. Golf is reckoned a silly game by many who perhaps do not understand it or have not tried it. It appeals to many of us because it offers us an opportunity to express certain basic urges—hitting long distances, shaping a shot into a wooded glen, or braving a steep chasm. And, wherever we humans may rank on the genetic scale, we are hardly ever satisfied in what we do because we feel there is always room for improvement. Put the other way round, golf is almost unique in that it permits unlimited improvement for everyone, whether beginner or one of golf's great masters. The game is such that it urges us to better ourselves and makes clear with every single stroke that improvement, however tiny, is within our grasp if we will try. Paul Runyan was determined to improve his swing at age ninety-two, and Tommy Bolt said he was still getting a kick out of playing at the age of eighty-six when they came to inform him of his induction into the Hall of Fame. "I don't care how old you get, you never lose that desire," he told writer Bill Fields. "Every day I go out, I'm trying to improve." And these two fellows knew something about the subject.

In our own search for improvement, we naturally turn to those who know more about it than we do and usually try to follow their injunctions as best we can. This process usually begins with something basic like how to hold the club and moves step by step through a progression of so-called fundamentals, adding one upon the other as we go. This is the usual way, and it's a good way, particularly if we can add to the business a little spark of genius from somewhere within ourselves. But this is where we often go wrong. We can't connect the steps with our own faulty reason, perhaps, or we battle with our own uncertain talents.

We seek perfection, or at least that degree of perfection that is ours alone. A wise and adventurous fellow once observed: "Perfection is finally

French aviator and novelist Antoine de Saint-Exupery with his mechanic Andre Prevot in front of his plane in 1938. Saint-Exupery vanished on a wartime reconnaissance mission in 1944.

attained not when there is no longer anything to add, but when there is no longer anything to take away." We can call this the "X" factor after its author, French aviator Antoine de Saint-Exupery. "St. X" was a pioneer who explored unknown territories and altitudes in his role as a pilot for the mail service in the 1920s and 1930s and chronicled his adventures in several popular books. He was writing of flight, not of golf, but his insight rings true for other crafts, like writing, which he did quite a lot of, and golf. Saint-Exupery wrote: "Perfection results when invention touches hands with the absence of invention. The line which the human eye follows with effortless delight is a line that had not been invented but simply discovered; in the beginning, it had been hidden by nature and in the end found by the engineer."

If permitted a paraphrase, we might say that the golf swing is an uncertain blend of invention and absence of invention, of the part of us we call instinct, which may at first be hidden by nature and in the end found with the help of a wise teacher or those twin tyrants, experiment and experience.

It is the process of constantly reshaping and polishing something—in Saint-Exupery's case an airplane wing, and in our case the golf swing—until it conforms, more or less, with those lines of least resistance we call the laws of nature. "It is as if there were a natural law which ordains that, in achieving our end, we are destined to follow the sole, guiding principle of simplicity," he wrote, one way of expressing the goals we seek in golf.

TEACHING VS. LEARNING

Simplicity is not so easily discovered, however, and complexity is very often substituted, not only by ourselves but by teachers. As pupils, we may also carry more subtle faults within us. Tommy Armour pointed out that there's a big difference between wanting to be taught and wanting to learn. Armour gained a reputation as a teacher not only because of his record as a great player, but also because he had a fabulous eye and understood the value of making things simple. To be taught by a famous man like Armour in his day, or by Leadbetter today, we can infer, carries a certain cachet that may feed our ego as much as our defective skills, while the desire to learn can be satisfied by anyone who combines knowledge with an ability to communicate. In other words, Hank Johnson or John Gerring can help you as much as Butch Harmon or David Pelz or another teaching superstar.

Davis Love Jr. had come to the same conclusion as Armour before his untimely death in an airplane crash. Love was a fine player and possibly America's most promising teacher, who had blended the wisdom of Harvey Penick, his mentor at college, John Jacobs, Bob Toski, and others with his own, very homey and practical insights. "Being a great student means a lot more in learning than having a great teacher," Davis said. "You can only be taught as well as you are willing to learn." He would have said that with a wry smile, ready with just the right words to encourage you to listen.

Tommy Armour became one of golf's most successful teachers after his playing days ended, and pointed out that there was a difference between wanting to be taught by a famous man and wanting to learn.

If your aspirations reach beyond your own to a son or daughter who seems to own a spark of talent, you might want to listen to the advice of Bob Murphy, a former U. S. Amateur champion, a veteran of both the regular and senior tours, and an occasional television commentator. Murphy

210

Earl Woods (right) and son, after Tiger won the 1991 Junior Amateur Championship in Orlando. Earl used to surprise Tiger by yelling during his swing or jumping out of closets to prepare him for the emotional trials of competitive golf.

told writer Nick Seitz that he had declined an offer of $5,000 to teach a youngster whose father wished to spare no expense in bringing the young fellow along. Instead, Murphy advised the man: "Take your son to several good golf courses in different parts of the country. Find different terrain, different grasses, different styles. Play the back tees and ask the superintendent to hide the pins. If the kid shoots 70 or better on every course, he might be a candidate. Then all he has to do is prove he can compete against all those other young tigers lurking in the jungle."

Today in the United States, there probably aren't more than three or four thousand kids between the ages of twelve and sixteen who can give a fellow like Murphy four a side and leave him begging for bus fare in the parking lot. Well, maybe only a thousand, but Bob Murphy's been around a while and knows what it takes to compete in the big time. So, my fellow zealots and tinkerers, if Jones was right about golf getting more difficult the longer we play it, why should we bother with any of this? Why not simply do as Armour and Burke advised—relax and smile, take an easy swipe at the ball, and let it go where it will? I suppose we all know the answer to that one.

BIBLIOGRAPHY

The Art of Golf, Sir Walter G. Simpson, David Douglas, Edinburgh, 1887.

Bobby Jones on Golf, Robert Tyre Jones, Doubleday, New York, 1966.

Bobby Locke on Golf, Bobby Locke, Country Life, London, 1953.

Chopin's Funeral, Benita Eisler, Alfred Knopf, New York, 2003.

The Complete Golfer, Harry Vardon, Metheun & Co. Ltd., London, 1905.

Concerning Golf, John L. Low (facsimile of 1903 edition), United States Golf Association, Far Hills, NJ, 1987.

The Decline and Fall of Practically Everybody, Will Cuppy, Henry Holt, New York, 1950.

The Dogged Victims of Inexorable Fate, Dan Jenkins, Little Brown, 1970.

The Encyclopedia of Golf, edited by Donald Steel and Peter Ryde, American editor Herbert Warren Wind, Viking, New York, 1975.

Fifty Years of Golf: My Memories, Andra Kirkaldy with Clyde Foster, E. P. Dutton & Co., New York, 1921.

Five Lessons: The Modern Fundamentals of Golf, Ben Hogan with Herbert Warren Wind, A. S. Barnes, New York, 1957.

The Game for a Lifetime, Harvey Penick with Bud Shrake, Simon & Schuster, New York, 1996.

The Game of Golf, Willie Park Jr., Longmans Green, London, 1901.

The Gate to Golf, J. Douglas Edgar, Edgar & Co., St. Albans, England, 1920; reprinted privately by James Douglas Edgar, London, 1982.

Gaugin's Intimate Journals, Boni & Liveright, New York, 1921; reprinted by Dover Publications, Mineola, NY, 1997.

The Glorious World of Golf, Peter Dobereiner, Grosset & Dunlap, New York, 1973.

Golf, Bob MacDonald, The Wallace Press, Chicago, 1927.

Golf: A New Approach, Lloyd Mangrum, Whittlesey House/ McGraw Hill, New York, 1949.

Golf Is My Game, Robert Tyre (Bobby) Jones, Doubleday, New York, 1959.

Golf: My Life's Work, J. H. Taylor, Jonathan Cape, London, 1943.

The Golf Swing, Cary Middlecoff with Tom Michael, Prentice Hall, Englewood Cliffs, NJ, 1974.

Golf through the Ages: 600 Years of Golfing Art, Michael Flannery & Richard Leech, Golf Links Press, Fairfield, Iowa, 2004.

Golfer's Gold, Tony Lema with Gwilym Brown, Little, Brown, Boston, 1964.

Golfing Memories and Methods, Joyce Wethered, Hutchinson & Co. Ltd., London, 1934.

Great Golfers: Their Methods at a Glance, G. W. Beldam, Macmillan, London, 1904.

Great Shots, Robert Sommers and Cal Brown, Anaya, London, and Chartwell, New York, 1989.

Green Memories, Bernard Darwin, Hodder & Stoughton Ltd., London, 1928.

Hints on Golf, Horace Hutchinson, William Blackwood, London, 1886.

A History of Golf in Great Britain, Bernard Darwin, et al., Cassell & Co., London, 1952.

How to Feel a Real Golf Swing, Bob Toski and Davis Love Jr., with Robert Carney, Golf Digest/Random House, New York, 1988.

How to Play Golf, Harry Vardon, Metheun & Co. Ltd., London, 1912.

How to Play Golf, H. J. Whigham, Herbert S. Stone & Co., Chicago, 1897.

How to Play Your Best Golf All the Time, Tommy Armour, Simon & Schuster, New York, 1953.

Let 'er Rip, Gardner Dickinson, Longstreet Press, Atlanta, GA, 1994.

The Life of Samuel Johnson, James Boswell Esq., 9th edition, T. Cadell et al., London, 1822.

The Little Red Book, Harvey Penick with Bud Shrake, Simon & Schuster, New York, 1992.

The Lonsdale Library, vol. IX: The Game of Golf, Joyce and Roger Wethered, Bernard Darwin, et al., Seeley, Service & Co. Ltd., London, 1931.

Master Guide to Golf, Cary Middlecoff with Tom Michael, Prentice Hall, Englewood Cliffs, NJ, 1960.

The Master of Putting, George Low with Al Barkow, Atheneum, New York, 1983.

Mostly Golf, edited by Peter Ryde, Adam & Charles Black Ltd., London, 1976.

My Game and Yours, Arnold Palmer, Simon & Schuster, New York, 1965.

My Golfing Life, Harry Vardon, Hutchinson, London, 1933.

My Partner, Ben Hogan, Jimmy Demaret, McGraw Hill, New York, 1954.

The Mystery of Golf, Arnold Haultain, Macmillan, New York, 1910.

The Natural Way to Better Golf, Jack Burke with Charles Price, Hanover House, New York, 1954.

On Learning Golf, Percy Boomer, Alfred Knopf, New York, 1946.

Paul Runyan's Book for Senior Golfers, Paul Runyan, Dodd, Mead & Co., New York, 1962.

Power Golf, Ben Hogan, A. S. Barnes, New York, 1948.

Practical Golf, John Jacobs with Ken Bowden, Quadrangle, New York, 1972.

Progressive Golf, Harry Vardon, Hutchinson, London, 1920.

The Putter Book, Bob Rosburg, Golf Digest Books, Norwalk, CT, 1963.

Quick Cures for Weekend Golfers, John Jacobs with Dick Aultman, Simon & Schuster, New York, 1979.

The Search for the Perfect Swing, Alastair Cochran & John Stobbs, J. B. Lippincott Co., Philadelphia and New York, 1968.

Secrets of the Master, edited by Sidney L. Matthew, Sleeping Bear Press, Chelsea, MI, 1996.

Shape Your Swing the Modern Way, Byron Nelson with Larry Dennis, Golf Digest/Simon & Schuster, New York, 1976.

The Spirit of St. Andrews, Alister Mackenzie, Sleeping Bear Press, Chelsea, MI, 1995.

Tee Shots and Others, Bernard Darwin, Kegan Paul, Trench, Trubner & Co., London, 1911.

Thirty Years of Championship Golf, Gene Sarazen with Herbert Warren Wind, Prentice Hall, New York, 1950.

The Touch System for Better Golf, Bob Toski with Dick Aultman, Golf Digest Inc., Norwalk, CT, and Simon & Schuster, New York, 1971.

Vardon on Golf, afterword by Sam McKinlay, Classics of Golf, edited by Herbert Warren Wind and Robert Macdonald, Norwalk, CT, 1989.

Wind, Sand and Stars, Antoine de Saint-Exupery, translated by Lewis Galantiere from *Terre des hommes*, 1939; reprinted by Harcourt Brace, New York, 1967.

ACKNOWLEDGMENTS

The author thanks several people who got him thinking about the subject, and others for plain, old-fashioned help in getting the book done, although none but the author is responsible for any contradictions, disagreements, and honest errors:

Bob Toski, for his candor and persistence and half a lifetime of friendship;

John Jacobs, for his keen sight and insight, a life well spent, and more;

Paul Runyan, for years of feisty determination and for delving into parts of golf most of us never quite understood;

George Fazio, for his elegant swing, his generosity, and restlessly stubborn approach to golf and life;

Ken Bowden, for many courtesies, including reading the raw text and making many helpful suggestions;

Robert Sommers, for reviewing the manuscript and offering substantial corrections of style and fact;

Jack Burke Jr., for a whole lot of common sense and a delightfully wicked sense of humor;

Judy Dickinson, for permission to quote from her late husband, Gardner's, book, *Let 'er Rip*.

For researching facts and tracking leads, Carol McCue, A. J. "Bert" Wright, Hubby Habjan, John Fite, Dick Janusch, Jack Hershey,

Joe Johnson, Tony Zitelli, John Mehigan, and Mark Brown. For permission to use rare photographs, Mac Hunter and Gordon "Joe" Ewen. For help with photo searches, Kelly Elbin and Lauren Cobb of The PGA of America, and Michael Salmon of AAF. And finally, special thanks to Jenna Brandon for valuable editorial suggestions.

PHOTO CREDITS

Amateur Athletic Foundation of Los Angeles 2 (both), 35, 37 (right), 71, 91, 117 (left), 204

Courtesy of Arnold Palmer Enterprises 32

Associated Press 7, 17, 53 (right), 69, 83, 132, 138, 194 (both)

Getty Images 14, 48, 52, 53 (left), 60, 61, 62, 63, 86, 94, 96, 107, 114, 117 (right), 144, 152 (left), 168, 174, 178, 189, 191, 208

Courtesy of Cal Brown 164

Courtesy of Jack Burke, Jr. 24 (left)

Courtesy of CBS Sports 110

Corbis Images 115, 127, 211

John Notar-Francesco 201 (diagram)

Courtesy of Indian Hill Club 25 (right)

Historic Golf Prints, Ron Watts Collection 3, 37 (left), 67, 72 (both), 85, 88, 89, 103, 116, 118, 143, 145, 152 (right), 157, 159, 160, 170, 173, 180, 184, 187, 196

The Mac Hunter Collection 24 (right), 34, 75, 210

Courtesy of John Jacobs 186

Courtesy of Scott Sayers 4

The PGA of America 47, 161

Phil Sheldon Library (Dale Concannon Collection) 5, 12, 21, 66, 99, 125, 149, 163, 176 (both), 206

Schickler Arts Gallery, Vintage Golf Collection 28, 39, 177

Courtesy of Bob Toski 27, 56, 199

United States Golf Association 25 (left)

INDEX

A